IN THIS
Light

Thoughts for Christmas

Archbishop of Canterbury
Justin Welby
and Friends

INSP:RE

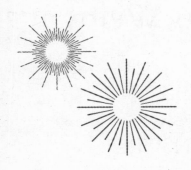

Acknowledgements

I am so grateful to those who have given their time to create *In This Light*.

Becoming Archbishop has given me untold privileges, one of which has been to meet and spend time with these wise friends and colleagues. Each of them has enriched my life and work, and this book fulfils my hope to share some of their words with you.

With my most sincere thanks to Arabella Mates, Rose Sandy, Rupert Grey and Helena Hayden-Cadd without whom this precious collection of messages would not have been shared.

I continue to hold John Cantlie in my prayers, brother of my dear friend Jessica. I am praying that somehow light reaches him this Christmas.

✦**The Most Revd Justin Welby**
Archbishop of Canterbury

It might not be the right time to pick up a book.

Who has time or space before Christmas for such luxury as sitting down and reading?

Even if you are a list person, chances are you don't get around to everything on the list, and there's little chance that giving yourself time to sit and read will even make it on to the list.

But the book you hold in your hand is not meant as another thing demanding your time. Another must before Christmas.

I am so grateful to those who have written something expressing their own individual and particular view of the light they see in our world, especially at Christmas. As you will quickly see, they are an eclectic bunch – believers and sceptics, priests, teachers and artists – each of whom has shaped how I think and work.

My prayer is that in receiving these words, your heart is filled with joy, hope and encouragement. That you receive the extravagant gift which defines Christmas; the one who is the Word made flesh, God with us, Jesus of Nazareth.

That we each hear our invitation to live in His light.

Wishing you all a very happy Christmas

Tash.

Perhaps the rapidly changing nature of work in the twenty-first century is not diminishing the importance of celebrations like Christmas, but making them even more special. Cheap travel, the internet, powerful mobile phones and other connected technologies, although certainly important milestones in human achievement, have made it all too easy to be distracted, to work longer hours, to spend more time on the road or abroad, and to allow business that might ordinarily remain in the office to creep into family life.

But there are also upsides to the tech revolution. The world is a much smaller place than it used to be even five or ten years ago. It's much easier today to stay connected to friends and family, even those you're unable to see regularly in person.

Nearly everyone has access to messaging apps to send Christmas wishes at the touch of a button. There are tools on nearly everyone's phone or computer to be able to video-chat with loved ones all over the world. There are fantastic initiatives online to help alleviate loneliness among the hundreds of thousands in Britain who feel this most acutely during this time. One is called #JoinIn, a conversation on Twitter on Christmas Day, to give company and support to those you might not know, wherever they are.

Whichever way you plan to connect this Christmas – through Christmas cards, over dinner, via video, or in church – make sure you put the technology aside for a few hours. Make the most of what's really important: spending time with those you love.

✛Matt Brittin
President EMEA Business and Operations, Google

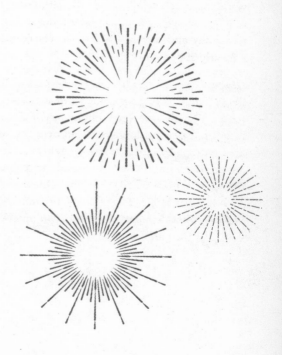

Every Wednesday afternoon I help lead a discussion group in the chapel of a London prison. Some men in the group you get to know very well. Others will just show up, say nothing and then disappear again. But every week, without fail, the conversation will go to a raw place that gives a glimpse of lost and broken hearts that are normally hidden behind strength and bravado.

Recently a man in our group told us that he didn't mind being in prison over Christmas, in fact he has enjoyed his best Christmas Days behind bars. I found this both sad and fascinating. Knowing a little of how bleak life in this particular prison can be, I thought, 'What sort of life must he have on the outside to love it in here?'

Then I thought of something else I hear mentioned in my group a lot: being imprisoned has nothing to do with being inside a jail. Unhealthy mindsets, addictions, shame, pride and selfishness are the sorts of things that bind us no matter where we are. Most repeat offenders understand this very well, so what hope do they have to ever find real freedom?

Some of the men have shown me that it is possible. One guy who is facing a long sentence told me a story of something that happened to him on the wing outside

his cell one afternoon. He was approached by another inmate who said, 'Aren't you one of those Christians? Someone told me if you go to chapel and follow Jesus you feel like you're free even when you're stuck in here. Is that true?' He assured the other inmate that it was since, when he was on the outside with all the material things he could ever want, he'd never come close to feeling as free as he did now, knowing Jesus.

Sadly, it's rare that men I know find this same freedom. There are challenges leaving prison: not just accommodation and employment, but loneliness and judgement from society, as well as the temptation to make quick money... The allure of a prison's comforts and the strong attachments to your former life are just a small part of it.

So when someone disappears, relapses or goes back inside, should we just give up? No. I think we're called to love, support and mentor – no matter what. Sometimes we have the wrong expectations or intentions and we just want a nice, shiny story of transformation. But when it's not glamorous and things don't seem to be working, I'm still encouraged by my friend's faith that shows me what real freedom looks like: a simple trust in Jesus and knowing you are loved by him, regardless of life's circumstances. I need more of that. This Christmas I'll be praying for that kind of freedom for my friends stuck inside jail and also the ones walking around on the outside.

✦**Luke Carson**

Brothers and sisters,

Once again, people are gathered all over the world to celebrate the life of Jesus Christ our Saviour; that sacred day of Christmas when we get to sing 'Joy to the World' for the child is born. Through his birth, the Lord entered into our humanity. In his birth, we are introduced to a unique way of God's love for all people, irrespective of gender and race. It is love in a world in need of peace and dignity for all. This love of God, shown in sending his Son to redeem the world, is a reminder that as human beings our journey on earth is for a short time.

As we celebrate, light candles, dance to wonderful songs and eat our favourite delicacies, let's not forget to embrace the love that comes with Christ's birth. Let us open our hearts to him so he may be born in us. Let us prayerfully examine our lives so we seek to build stronger relationships with him – and with our neighbours.

It's my prayer and hope that we let love and compassion reign for all children and women who are injured, deprived, hungry, homeless and hopeless; especially in the war-torn parts of the Middle East, Democratic Republic of Congo, South Sudan, Somalia, Yemen, Israel/Palestine, Venezuela, Colombia, and many more. May solidarity, hospitality and love be our light during this season. Let the tyrant regimes that continue to oppress their people experience repentance, forgiveness and mercy as the light of Christ transforms their attitudes and behaviour.

Brothers and sisters, our world is wounded. Our people are fractured and on the move. The logic of development, and its methods, are marked by exclusion and environmental degradation. Christ's birth calls on us to love each other – because it is through love that the whole world can be healed. May Christmas bestow upon us a renewed desire to build future societies founded on values of empathy, love, dignity, solidarity, joy and hope.

Let the Christmas light of hope and love shared by Jesus Christ bring joy and peace!

✚ Dr Agnes Abuom
Moderator, World Council of Churches Central Committee

The people who walked in darkness
*   have seen a great light;*
those who lived in a land of deep darkness –
*   on them light has shined…*
For a child has been born for us,
*   a son given to us;*
authority rests upon his shoulders;
*   and he is named*
Wonderful Counsellor, Mighty God,
*   Everlasting Father, Prince of Peace.*
His authority shall grow continually,
*   and there shall be endless peace*
for the throne of David and his kingdom.
*   He will establish and uphold it*
with justice and with righteousness
*   from this time onward and forevermore.*
The zeal of the Lord of hosts will do this.

Isaiah 9: 2, 6–7 (NRSV)

I first met Maram during Christmas 2016.

Christmas Eve had started disappointingly. I walked into the recovery ward before dawn, looking for this baby girl of five months, on whom I had operated the day before. I was leaving Syria that morning and wanted to see her before I left.

Maram's mother and father had been killed going through one of the crossing points to West Aleppo, as the siege of the eastern part of the city drew to a close that month. She had terrible injuries from fragmentation wounds to her leg, hand and arm, and could easily have died without proper wound management. I worried that her injuries were too serious for her to survive, but we did as much as we could.

I went to find Maram just before I crossed the border back to Turkey. I scoured the wards but she was not there. Some of the doctors and nurses I spoke to knew nothing about her, so I assumed the worst. When I got back to London, I drove straight down to Devon to meet my family, finally arriving at three in the morning. That Christmas Day, as I held my wife and daughter close, I counted my blessings.

I received a call from the BBC a few months later; they had found Maram and she was safe and well. It was a little late for Christmas, but it was the greatest gift imaginable.

✦ **David Nott**
Cofounder of the David Nott Foundation and
Professor of Conflict Surgery, Imperial College London

I have some unforgettable memories of Christmas.

In the 1990s, I escaped North Korea in search of religious freedom. For several years after I crossed the border, I was afraid of being captured and deported to North Korea. In those suffering years, I was able to visit a house church where I could study the Bible and learn hymns. There I heard about Christmas for the first time. I had never had a Christmas in North Korea.

Christmas is the birthday of Jesus Christ, the only Son of God, who died on the cross for my sins. I had no words to express my joy as I celebrated my first Christmas Day. The Holy Spirit came to me and changed my sorrow to overflowing joy. I sang worship songs every day and was so happy to study the Bible. I had so many reasons to be thankful to God. Even though I had nothing in my hands, I felt so happy because Jesus was with me.

After that, I was captured and deported back to North Korea twice. I was imprisoned and tortured because I shared the Gospel with other prisoners. In every moment, the Holy Spirit was with me to protect, comfort and strengthen me. In the last prison where I was detained, I built a secret church with several other prisoners to worship our heavenly God. We held a small, quiet worship service in the prison toilet, because no guards would come near there.

While I was praying and worshipping silently, Jesus Christ gave me a Christmas poem. Jesus never forgot me. He comforted me and strengthened my heart to be courageous.

After three years in that prison — a place where there was no hope and several people died every day — I was released, with the helping hands of God.

2 Samuel 7: 9 (NRSV) says: 'I have been with you wherever you went, and have cut off all your enemies from before you; and I will make for you a great name, like the name of the great ones of the earth.' I believed the promise of God and that his blessings would come after my sufferings. He strengthened me and I miraculously survived the valley of the shadow of death. Now I live in South Korea where there is religious freedom.

Every Christmas, I remember his amazing grace and blessings. I feel so happy because many Christian believers all over the world pray for people like me.

I pray that North Korean believers can one day freely celebrate Christmas Day by worshipping and laughing together in North Korea. I will sing the Christmas songs and pray out loud with all my heart and mind until God answers our prayers.

✦**Hea Woo**
Member of a North Korean underground church

Today is Christmas Day!

A Christmas poem by Hea Woo

Today is Christmas Day
When our Jesus was born,
Jesus who died on the cross for me.
Let us worship Him
With all our hearts and minds,
With joyful songs to worship Jesus.

Today is Christmas Day
When our Jesus was born.
Jesus who poured out His blood on the cross.
Let us sing
His amazing love and grace,
With joyful songs to worship Jesus.

One day, on a a twelve-hour flight, I watched a very famous film which children love: *Spiderman*. At one point, there is a tragic situation. The hero makes a last-ditch attempt to try and save a crowd-filled train heading straight towards a collapsed bridge above a chasm. Then we see amazing pictures of Spiderman jumping from house to house and standing right in front of the locomotive engine, facing the chasm, opening his arms and painfully stopping the whole train with his body. Of course he succeeds right at the edge of the chasm. As he leaves, there is a cross-shaped mark left by his body on the train from the strain of his effort.

From that day, on numerous flights, I have noticed with joy that great films with worldwide success are always, without exception, films where the main character risks and even lays down his life for others.

I thought about Jesus' saying in the Scriptures: 'No one has greater love than this, to lay down one's life for one's friends' (John 15: 13 NRSV). As I watched other films, such as the Narnia movies, *Ice Age* (when the good mammoth gives his life for his enemy, the tiger), *Avatar*, *The Lord of the Rings*, *E.T.*, I thought that Jesus' message and the message of Christmas are received more and more by non-believers as much as by believers. Yes indeed, there is no greater love than to lay down one's life for one's friends.

✦**Father Laurent Fabre**
Founder of the Chemin Neuf Community, an international Catholic community with an ecumenical vocation

Gentleness has been my watchword this year. I hold this quality in deep reverence.

It is love in action in a uniquely beautiful way. Gentleness is listening without charging in with advice. It's holding a hand. It's sighing empathetically. Gentleness is an act of service done with no need for acknowledgement or even knowing. It's a calm steadiness. It's a loving presence we all long to be in and have within.

Yet it seems in recent years that extroversion, visible success, noisy activism, assertive confidence (all noble and necessary qualities for some and in some walks of life) have pushed gentleness into the background. So much so that some people now misalign gentleness with laziness, or shyness, or seem to think that gentle people are less important people.

Give me gentle any day, particularly at Christmas, a time of year when we are celebrating love – beautiful, tender, gentle love. But what are actually we doing? Rushing. Feeling fraught about all the 'shoulds' and 'musts'.

Well, I invite you to stop amid this whirlwind of Christmas tunes and bright flashing lights, and consider a gentler approach. Slow your pace. Listen first of all to your heart and be tender with your own needs. Yes, your own — imagine that! And as you feel fuelled by the energy you gain from doing this, gently listen, empathise and give.

Isn't that what we really want to feel, remember, and be? Isn't that what is important, more than looking good at the right parties, organising a fifteen-course meal you don't want to cook or even eat, or having perfectly behaved kids in the perfect nativity?

Take the pressure off. Who on earth are we trying to impress anyway? Go gently. I venerate gentleness and I wish the world did a bit more too.

✦**Miranda Hart**
Actress, writer and comedian

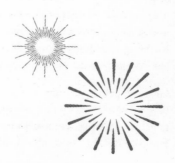

I have turned 37 years old. The only noteworthy thing about this is the fact that it is my first adult year of not being a rower. Hanging up my oar after a career spanning five Olympiads comes as something of a relief. I have enjoyed so many ups and endured even more downs and I finally realise, in this time of stormy transition, that sport is a wonderful metaphor for life.

Rowing was a wonderful time, but also an enduring struggle. It was constant work, preparation, pressure, assessment and competition. It was brutal and relentless. It could feel very lonely. I was often lying on the floor in my own pool of sweat. I had to weather storms alone. The team suffered setbacks. The coach was never satisfied. The boat was known to break.

I always did my best to pick myself up, often aided by a boost from my crew. In turn, I made every effort to lift those around me when they struggled and I had my strength to inspire them. In the hardest times we handled ourselves with honour, integrity and kindness. In sport and in life, the greatest of these virtues is kindness.

A final thought: in all those years I didn't ever have a perfect row. Perfect isn't real and real isn't perfect. We aimed for small improvements and the satisfaction wasn't in the gold medal; it came from the daily joy of working with those around us, to make small and progressive steps, with a light heart.

✦**Lieutenant Pete Reed, OBE, Royal Navy**
Olympic champion 2008, 2012, 2016

Beyond the tinsel and the tree, Christmas is a time for joy and a call to love; a season where we walk a little lighter and try a little harder to spread love outwards beyond the walls of kith and kin. But more than that, it is a time to find the full meaning in God's gift of an innocent infant born in a stable.

Easter brings its own meaning and its own powerful lessons. But anyone who has ever wrestled with the meaning of faith can find much inspiration in the act of love required for God to send his innocent Son to walk among us, as one of us, knowing all that would follow. Likewise we can gain inspiration from the extraordinary Gospel of Jesus, who taught us that 'the Son of Man came not to be served but to serve, and to give his life a ransom for many' (Matthew 20: 28 NRSV).

Over many years, through a war and through the loss of friends and the suffering of family, my faith has experienced highs and lows. All the questions asked millions of times by millions of people before came to mind – none brilliant or original, but earnest, heartfelt and genuine. How can there be a merciful God who allows this carnage to take place? How does God choose between one child and another, as to who lives or dies?

If I watched a day's worth of college football post-game interviews, I would hear again and again that God had a 'plan' to help quarterbacks win victories; by the time the evening news rolled around, was I supposed to believe that God had no plan for kids starving in Africa? Was this God's will? Sometimes, in our rush to have God take sides in trivial things, we miss entirely the places where God might really be seen, or the reasons we might not see him present at all.

What brought me a certain kind of peace about my faith finally arrived after reading and rereading Pope John Paul II's Apostolic Letter on 'salvific suffering'. It reminded me of the words of St Paul that I had heard so many times in catechism: 'In my flesh I am completing what is lacking in Christ's afflictions for the sake of his body, that is, the church' (Colossians 1: 24 NRSV). His Holiness pointed to the Old Testament, where Job's suffering was God's punishment. He contrasted it with the New Testament, where God didn't save his only Son from suffering but gave him eternal life to end suffering – all in return for Jesus putting his faith in the Father.

All of it, any of it, possible only because God loved us so much, so unconditionally, that he had given his only Son to the flesh. How extraordinary. This gift we remember and renew each Christmas through the story of a tiny baby away in a manger.

✦John F. Kerry
Sixty-eighth US Secretary of State

24

My great-grandparents were born into slavery in America and over the last few years I've been preoccupied with trying to understand how they survived. How did they endure the bondage, objectification, degradation, abuse, assaults and trauma of enslavement?

My grandparents lived in the American South when racial terrorism and lynching shaped the lives of black people. African Americans were drowned, beaten, burned, hanged and tormented by white mobs for decades; millions had to flee the region as refugees and exiles. How did they persevere? My parents grew up in apartheid and racial segregation. They were denied opportunities for education, employment, fair housing; they were often excluded, humiliated and marginalised.

Yet, I was born to people with great hope.

My elders taught me to believe that hopelessness is the enemy of justice. I was told that the absence of hope will cause you to accept inequality, bigotry, discrimination and oppression in ways that cannot be reconciled with redemption and restoration. Hope is critical if we want a more just world: you're either hopeful or you become part of the problem. I was told that sometimes I would have to stand up when others told me to sit down. I was warned that sometimes I would have to speak when others were telling me to be quiet. My people told me that hope is my superpower, and that hope can lead you to love.

Nothing is better than love.

I've come to understand that my ancestors survived because they understood the power of love to overcome the torment and anguish of inequality. They understood that they had to fight against the brutality and violence of bigotry, without ever losing hope and giving up on love. Because love is the way to joy, mercy, compassion and redemption.

And so, I have been taught to stay on the side of love – because without love there is violence and despair that will not end.

Today I work with the condemned, the imprisoned, the poor, the excluded, the marginalised and the disfavoured; I advocate for the addicted, disabled, traumatised and neglected. I am often frustrated, often challenged, but I am hopeful. I feel the strength of my ancestors. I get to witness God's grace. I am resolved to stay on the side of love … it is a blessing.

✦ **Bryan Stevenson**
Founder and Executive Director, Equal Justice Initiative

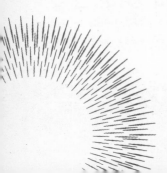

Tehran, Christmas 1983 – a young Muslim boy on a bicycle was stopped in his tracks. Singing was coming from a church, and this boy found himself climbing the wall to catch a glimpse of what was inside. People were busily decorating a tree, cleaning and polishing the tables and pews, and arranging furniture. In the centre of all this, five young girls in white robes were practising songs of praise. Christians preparing for Christmas Day. The marvellous arches of this church hugged the houses on either side, and there this boy sat, hypnotised.

I was that young boy. I can say that on that night I was really and truly touched by what I had seen and heard. Christmas was more than Santa, more than presents. Something that I – a Muslim never invited to a Christmas service or party of any kind – could join.

I have not seen that church wall, or my homeland, since 2011. I fled when it became impossible to be a Christian and to worship freely there. I have been in England for most of that time; heartbroken for what I have lost, what I continue to lose through separation, but filled with gratitude, and with hope, by the welcome I have received.

St Margaret's Church, Easter 2015. Father Stephen asked me to carry the Easter Candle: to walk in my robe up to the altar and declare that Lord Jesus is the light of the world. Truly, I was more moved than I can say: so, so proud that I – a refugee, an outsider – was now literally part of the Church of England.

Lambeth Palace, Christmas time. Without doubt it was an amazing invitation. I couldn't believe it. And, even more than that, I was asked to be one of the readers. It was an evening I will never forget – singing no longer heard by climbing up a wall, but enjoyed freely and safely. This is where my Lord had taken me. Though so far from my own land, I was safe and among Christians and convinced more than ever that Jesus asked us to love each other.

Christmas now means a lot to that young boy. What our God expects are not just words and pleasant thoughts, but also deeds every single day. Welcome freely, celebrate openly and love without condition. Worship, like those girls' beautiful singing, is something we can all join. Whether you're in hiding in Iran, living at Lambeth Palace, or anywhere else in the world, I am sending you my prayers. Happy Christmas.

✦Benjamin
Iranian refugee
Member of the Church of England and the British community

I first began to appreciate Christmas when I was 7 years old. Though I was living in Southern Sudan, far away from the winter wonderland and flying reindeers that symbolise Christmas in the West, there was one thing I'm sure we *all* looked forward to come Christmas time – the gifts. This was the one time of year when we would get things we never got the rest of the year: sweets, biscuits, clothes and whatever else our family could afford.

In our new Christmas clothes, already stained and sticky with sweets, families across the town would come together in church; where we prayed, celebrated and feasted. In a country where the struggle for independence had become a part of our daily reality, there was no doubt that this was a special time of year.

When South Sudan gained its independence in 2011, I hoped that the people would be able to celebrate, in abundance, the many Christmases that they had missed during the Struggle. A Christmas without gunshots or fear; a Christmas with security and love. But it did not happen that way for us. December 2013 was the beginning of a long period of despair for most South Sudanese people. That year there would be no Christmas and there has been little to celebrate since.

From that time, as each Christmas passes I find myself thinking about those who live in refugee camps, in the bush, and in the diaspora who have no country to return to – the forlorn and the abandoned South Sudanese all over the world. This Christmas, like many others, South Sudanese will gather in church with their hearts heavy and pray that the Son of God will one day see their suffering.

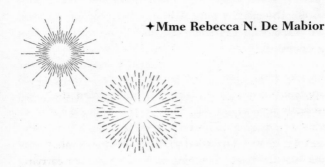

✦Mme Rebecca N. De Mabior

Here is my servant, whom I uphold,
my chosen, in whom my soul delights;
I have put my spirit upon him;
he will bring forth justice to the nations.
He will not cry or lift up his voice,
or make it heard in the street;
a bruised reed he will not break,
and a dimly burning wick he will not quench;
he will faithfully bring forth justice.
He will not grow faint or be crushed
until he has established justice in the earth;
and the coastlands wait for his teaching.

Isaiah 42: 1–4 (NRSV)

All of us have mixed experiences of Christmas. Some of us may love it, but many of us dread Christmas Day and even the anticipation and build-up. It can be a really hard time due to lack of family support, sorely missing loved ones, and the pressure to find money to buy the perfect gifts. We may look around and feel we don't have the same picture-perfect Christmas as everyone else.

In our Bible study group at Charis, as Christmas approaches, we try to explore together what the point of Jesus' birth really was. Mary has really stood out to us all – a teenage girl chosen by God to bring his Son into this world. We have tried to imagine what it must have felt like for Mary. Claiming to be a virgin but carrying God's child must have been difficult. How would you not worry that no one would believe you? How would you not worry that you had lost the plot and made the whole thing up? How would you even prove you were telling the truth? We discovered Mary was at risk of being rejected in society for the rest of her life. Then we see her bravery and how she chose to follow God even though it was really difficult and costly for her.

At Charis we found this inspiring and challenging. It left us wondering: how can we as a community follow God when it feels risky, hard and beyond our capabilities? Especially when it feels like something those around us might disapprove of.

How can we let God use us even when we don't trust that we would be the best choice?

At times for us it feels impossible to be close to God because of all the things that feel so complicated and hard in life. The Christmas story reminds us that God uses the unlikely – not those who society may think are the best choice or the strongest candidate. When we feel as if we aren't good enough or strong enough to be used by God, we can remember the great risk Mary took and how hard that must have felt at times for her. It reminds us that as we take risks in trying to do the right thing, God is with us and doesn't want us to feel afraid or alone. It reminds us this Christmas that, as painful as the complexities of life are, we have a God who will see us through them and give us the courage we need.

This Christmas we will have hope.

✦**Written together by the Charis Tiwala community**
Charis Tiwala is a charity supporting
people exploited or affected by the sex industry

Christmas tells us that God is close. Some may not believe in God at all, whereas others believe he exists yet consider him to be distant and uninterested. But the Christmas story tells us something altogether different. Here is a God who lays aside every conceivable advantage, and humbles himself to become both servant and Saviour. Here is the One whose footstool is the earth, and yet came to the earth to put himself in our shoes. Here is the voice that declared 'Let there be light' and yet somehow is heard in in the fragile cry of the newborn baby that was born on Christmas Day.

The Christmas narrative shows us a God we can identify with – and who identifies with us. The same blood, the same flesh, the same skin, the same breath. He is just as high and holy as He ever was – yet He is not remote, or unable to relate. As theologians Roger Olsen and Stanley Grenz remind us, God is 'immanent within human experience as the transcendent mystery that cannot be comprehended in spite of its absolute nearness'.

The wonderful truth of the Christmas message is that God has not left the building. He is intervening in our everyday lives. For our lonely moments, for our seasons of weakness, and for the times we battle through life wondering who is on our side, here he lies in a manger – Emmanuel, the God who is with us.

✦**Matt Redman**
Grammy Award-winning songwriter

I am writing this from one of the most peaceful places in the world: the Omani desert, where it is 45° C/113° F (hot!) and very, very quiet; not even the sound of birdsong. At night the temperature drops rapidly, campfires are lit, and light radiates from a million glittering stars.

I wonder if this is what it was like for the shepherds on the night Jesus was born. In the Gospel of Luke we read: 'And suddenly there was with the angel a multitude of the heavenly host praising God and saying, Glory to God in the highest heaven, and on earth peace among those whom he favours' (Luke 2: 13–14 NRSV).

It is not often we experience peace on earth. We live in a world more intent on talking than listening, fighting than loving. Our friends and colleagues in South Sudan witness such conflict day after day. Many of them have never known life without violence. We don't have to look that far to see the impact of conflict. We know too well the fallout from fighting in our personal relationships at home, work, church and school. There has been remarkably little peace on earth throughout the history of humanity.

Imagine the shock of the shepherds when their desert peace was shattered by bright lights and heavenly voices. And their surprise when they heard the words of praise, proclaiming peace instead of the unrest they knew existed beyond their campfire. How did they respond? They left their flocks to seek Jesus, the source of peace on earth.

St Paul writes: 'In Christ, God was reconciling the world to himself, not counting their sins against them' (2 Corinthians 5: 19 NRSV). Through Jesus, and on the night he was born, God was acting to draw us closer to himself. The whole of Jesus' life was testimony to this reconciling act. From his very first encounter with the shepherds as a baby, Jesus met, ate, spoke and lived with the outcasts of his day, those whom others saw as unacceptable to God.

The angel of the Lord did not announce the arrival of Jesus to all the world. He chose a little group of shepherds huddled round a single campfire. Then and now, the message of peace was spread person to person. From the angels to the shepherds, to the people they met on their journey, and beyond.

We too are called to testify to God's reconciling act, drawing us closer to himself, the one in whom true peace is found. We are commissioned as ambassadors of Christ and ministers of reconciliation. To share the Prince – and promise – of Peace in our personal relationships; listening instead of talking, loving instead of fighting. It is rarely an easy journey, especially with those we find hardest to love, but it leads us to the Prince of Peace. In him alone, we discover peace on earth.

✛**Canon Sarah Snyder**
The Archbishop of Canterbury's Adviser for Reconciliation

I wonder if there has ever been a more difficult time to admit that one believes in God.

Churches are certainly filled in times of crisis, but for the rest of the time most of us bumble along with our faith – if we have one – tucked at the back of the mind; to be hauled out when all else fails.

At the church youth club I attended as an angst-ridden lad, we had a visit from the then Bishop of Wakefield, Eric Treacy. I asked how we could prove that God existed. He smiled sympathetically, shrugged and said, 'We cannot. That is why it is called faith. We cannot see it, but we can believe it.'

The family faith in which I grew up was low Anglican – no candles and (perish the thought) certainly no incense. My father was in the church choir and my mother was enrolling member of the Mothers' Union, but they regarded this as a normal, unremarkable part of their lives. That kind of faith has remained a part of my own life. Presenting the BBC's *Songs of Praise* and two Sunday evening series on worship in the 1980s and '90s, I endeavoured to act as a sympathetic 'Everyman' rather than a tub-thumping theologian.

I have always been more comfortable demonstrating my faith in a quiet way, unable and unwilling to declare blithely that God will sort out everything. He probably will, but not always in a way that is either predictable or comfortable. And sometimes he needs a bit of help from mere mortals.

'God is love,' we were taught at Sunday school. To me, that love manifests itself most frequently through the beauty of the natural world and through the life-enhancing people I meet. They may not necessarily be devout, or exhibit an unreal aura of serenity, but in them I detect a goodness which is just helpful and enriching, and frequently founded on Christian principles.

At a time when we supposedly have a greater understanding of the universe and our place within it, it is all too easy to sniff at faith – a belief in something that seems to defy reason, logic, science and human omnipotence. And yet when I look into my grandchildren's eyes, or walk in the garden or countryside, I find the kind of magic and wonder that reinforces my belief in God. 'Ah!' cry the cynics. 'There is not an ounce of proof that such feelings have anything to do with God.' Maybe not, but they have everything to do with faith.

It is not easy for most of us to articulate our complex feelings about the meaning of life; but that should not undermine – nor cause to be undervalued – a faith that manifests itself in a love of nature and in the loving kindness and consideration we can show one another. It is this kind of 'love in action' that has the ability, little by little, to improve the world in which we live – not always on a global scale, but certainly to that part of the world closest to us.

That, to me, is at the heart of civilised human existence, and at the heart of my own Christian faith. It is not always easy to live up to, but it is definitely worth aiming for.

✦Alan Titchmarsh MBE
Gardener, novelist, writer and broadcaster

Christmas reminds many Christians about the birth of Jesus Christ, the Prince of Peace.

Around 4 BC, there were wise men ready to receive Jesus' birth with joy and gifts. The nation of Israel was not as prepared as the wise men, because it was not only under the leadership of Imperial Rome but was also full of crimes and wickedness. There was strife all over. Its people suffered calamity under King Herod's hand as a result of the Saviour's birth.

December 2013 wasn't the time for South Sudanese to receive the Prince of Peace as wise men. It was when it became clear that the nation, like Israel in 4 BC, had for too long been trapped by too many evils. Peace was wounded then, and remains fragile now.

Those who thrive in chaos and conflict chased peace out of our country. If it is to return, wise men and women will have to work hard – work to heal conflicts, bridge divides, and prepare us once more for a peaceful, joyful South Sudan. It is these wise peacemakers I choose to join.

To be a peacemaker is to believe that our Saviour Jesus Christ, who personified peace, is the most powerful force on earth: just as he escaped Herod and then death, rising again, so will we overcome the evils that too often rampage through our country. To be a peacemaker is to believe that we will make Christmas joyous again in South Sudan.

✦**Emmily Koiti**
Medical doctor
Peace and rights activist

In the chill of winter, at the end of another year of upheaval and uncertainty, the glow of a glorious summer seems a world away.

But as we reflect this Christmas on the year that is almost over, we surely won't forget the heady month of July and two stories that – for a few short days – took us away from our political and social divisions and made us look up.

The decency and modesty of the young England World Cup football team, who took us further than any had dreamed of, brought families together on sofas and communities out onto the streets in an outburst of joy we hadn't seen since the Olympics of 2012.

But as their matches played out to millions on the biggest stage in sport, another football team was utterly hidden from world view: twelve Thai boys and their football coach trapped in the flooded depths of a two-mile long cave. Who didn't put themselves in the shoes of the families who waited in agony for news?

As the boys were brought out one by one, what unfolded was a story of quiet heroism and self-sacrifice …

The Royal Thai Navy diver who lost his own life in an attempt to save the boys.

The British cave experts who were central to the effort, awesome in their knowledge and bravery, but even more awesome in their humanity – gently coaxing and reassuring twelve boys who didn't speak their language and couldn't even swim.

The team of medics, engineers and military that descended on the remote hillside from around the world: an inspirational show of international cooperation, where borders and divisions melted away as tragedy seemed to draw near.

The rescue felt like a miracle. The families surely needed one. But maybe we all needed to witness it, to remind us what truly matters in life and what it means to be human.

✛Julie Etchingham
Journalist and mother of two

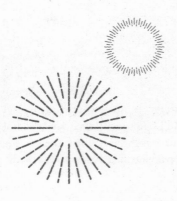

I have a gift for you.

For thirty years, my Christmas did not look like any Christmas you might read about in a book, watch on television, or hear about from a pulpit. There were no presents. There wasn't a feast of delicious food. There wasn't the comfort of family or the sound of children's laughter. For thirty years, Christmas Day was a tiny, dark, bleak room, made of mesh and cement and horror.

For thirty years, I spent Christmas on death row at Holman Prison in Alabama. I was an innocent man, locked in a cage, living a waking nightmare.

Christmas is not any different from any other day on death row. There is no decoration. No special meals. No Christmas service. No special visits from family or friends. For many men on death row, Christmas is just an extra painful day in a year of painful days spent waiting to die.

I learned in that dark place a few things that I'd like to share with you this holiday season. I learned that no one can take away your joy if you don't let them. If you find yourself feeling down during the holidays, as many do, you have the ability to use your mind to lift yourself to higher places. I survived death row by learning to leave death row in my mind. My mind allowed me to escape my circumstance. I also relied on my faith, believing that God had a plan for me and I had to trust that God did not fail. Whatever prison your mind has you in, believe me when I tell you it can be transcended and transformed.

I also learned that you always have a gift to give another person. Even the poorest, the most lost, the most marginalised and forgotten among us has the ability to reach out to another human and give comfort. Give time. Give them something to laugh about. 'I'm here for you' is a powerful prayer. Listening is free.

And finally, I learned that hope is everything. If I could wrap something up and put it under the Christmas tree for each and every one of you, it would be the small seed of hope that can grow into something mighty. If you are forsaken, I offer you hope as a lifeline. If you are forgotten, I shout hope into your name. If you are lost, I send you hope as navigation to finding your way home. If you feel unloved, I remind you that God loves you unconditionally on this day and on every day, and may you find the hope in that truth. May the small seed of hope I gift to you live under your skin and settle into your bones and find its place within your heart, so it takes root and both lifts you up and shows you that no matter the circumstance, you can always reach a hand out to lift another up.

My gift to you is the same gift that freed me from a hell on earth.

The gift of hope.

Pass it on.

✦**Anthony Ray Hinton**
Author, The Sun Does Shine

How does joy arrive? On a donkey. That speaks to me.

'Humour is, in fact, a prelude to faith; and laughter is the beginning of prayer,' said theologian Reinhold Niehbur. 'Laughter must be heard in the outer courts of religion, and the echoes of it should resound in the sanctuary.'

For me, Christmas represents faith and laughter. They have more in common than people think – they're both all about life's incongruities. The joy of the Christmas story comes in part from its absurdities. There's elating, anything-is-possible comic multiplication (not one impossible birth but *two* – and two prophets, both *women*) and the gleeful farce around John the Baptist's conception.

Jesus' first entrance can even seem comic. Malachi speaks of him with fear and trembling: 'But who can endure the day of his coming? Who can stand when he appears? For he will be like a refiner's fire.' … Pull back and reveal tiny, mute baby, arms and legs pinned to his sides with swaddling, perched inches from a cowpat. He's from

Nazareth, *the* joke town, and worshipped by shepherds, *the* joke profession of the time. The sublime wrapped up in the ridiculous. But just because something's ridiculous doesn't mean it isn't real, as any blobfish will attest.

I felt so exposed writing this that at my lowest point I genuinely considered plagiarising a Christmas message off the Pope. How ridiculous is that? But if Christmas tells us anything, it's that you don't need to be a pope to see angels. And this, of all the lessons in the world, is the one I ought to have learnt. I have lived with a child with Down's syndrome for a while now, and at night he talks to angels that I cannot see.

'God chose what is foolish in the world to shame the wise; God chose what is weak in the world to shame the strong' (1 Corinthians 1: 27 NRSV).

Most of my friends with Down's syndrome have both a profound faith and an acute sense of humour. Olly provides me with privileged access to a stream of comic absurdity and joy that is turned up to eleven at Christmas. He heads out Christmas shopping with his £6 burning a hole in his pocket. I get a call from Trailfinders. He's trying to buy a ticket to Perth. He parties hard, loves much, always wins the chocolate game and sings carols like a lovestruck sea cow. He forgives quickly, is always grateful and is the first to laugh at himself. He's so very free. I have an Oxford degree, a career I love, but at Christmas I realise he has something more precious.

It has been a mixed year for us in Down's syndrome Land (do visit, if you haven't — music, moonlight, love, etc.). We're working, getting married, winning medals and so on, but education has become less inclusive, not more, and the effects of austerity have hit all people with disabilities harder than any other group. The UK is under investigation by the UN Committee on the Rights of Persons with Disabilities and has been found guilty of serious human rights violations.

We were elated that the Church of England Synod considered the well-being of those with Down's syndrome. We give thanks for all who want to help us in the future. We welcome the British Medical Association debate on the ethics of the new prenatal 'Down's test' recently rolled out on the National Health Service. Initial freedom-of-information requests suggest that where the test has been available privately, the Down's syndrome birth rate has dropped, sometimes by much as 75 per cent.

Most people think that babies should be a gift not a commodity. Technologies like this prenatal Down's test, and gene editing, take us towards a consumerist ethos in obstetrics. I happen to believe that kids like Olly are the gift that keeps on giving. And if that's not a Christmas message, well, it's the best I can do.

✦**Sally Phillips**
Actress, comedian and writer

Last year I assisted at the midnight Christmas Mass presided over by Pope Francis at St Peter's Basilica. The moment arrived for the singing of the *Kalenda*, the solemn proclamation of the birth of the Saviour – a chant which was part of the ancient Martyrology and was reintroduced into the Catholic liturgy after Vatican II:

> *When ages beyond number had run their course from the creation of the world,*
>
> *in the thirteenth century since the People of Israel were led by Moses in the Exodus from Egypt;*
>
> *in the one hundred and ninety-fourth Olympiad;*
>
> *in the year seven hundred and fifty-two since the foundation of the City of Rome;*
>
> *in the forty-second year of the reign of Caesar Octavian Augustus,*
>
> *Jesus Christ, eternal God and Son of the eternal Father, was conceived by the Holy Spirit, and when nine months had passed since his conception, was born of the Virgin Mary in Bethlehem of Judah, and was made man.*

When the last words were said, I felt a sudden inner clarity; I remember saying to myself: 'It is true! Everything they are singing is true! These are not just words; the Eternal actually has entered into time. The last event of the series has broken the series; it has created an irreversible "before" and "after"; the computation of time, which took place earlier in relation to different events (the Olympics, such and such a kingdom, and so on), now takes place in relation to a single event — the birth of a baby in a poor village of a despised Roman province!'

A sudden emotion shot through my entire person, and I could only say, 'Thank you, Most Holy Trinity, and thanks be also to you, Holy Mother of God.'

✝**Father Raniero Cantalamessa**
Preacher to the Papal Household in Rome

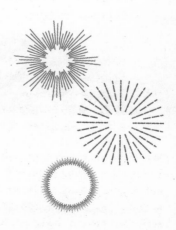

In July, I was drawing in a Syrian refugee camp, Domiz 1, in northern Iraq. The camp is seven years old, and homes have turned from tents to concrete and tin. The wedding dress shop was open that day. The fridge-mender was working away while his children, Laila and Asad, ran around offering drinks. The fruit-shop man on the corner handed me a box of plums in an embarrassing gesture of generosity. Many, despite their abhorrent recent history, now consider this home.

A week earlier and sixty kilometres south, I drew in West Mosul. It was ten months since the defeat of Islamic State (IS). Mohammed had opened this shop two weeks earlier, selling falafel sandwiches among the rubble to those trying to rebuild their homes. The bulldozers across the road demolished a bombed-out car park, Neshwan

A new falafel shop in West Mosul, July 2018.
George Butler

opened a hardware store, and 15-year-old Idris dug new wells with his uncle in an attempt to bring water back to some of the old city.

Here, there is no avoiding the brutal upheaval that has been forced upon many in Syria and Iraq; unwilling hosts to war. In some cases, they have lost everything they have ever known. There is still so much to do, but as I was reminded this summer, human nature doesn't need much to get a foothold. And if our intention in the West is indeed to help, then that is what we should strive for. The alternatives – indifference, apportioning blame, and denying the narratives that don't complement our own – are equally destructive to those in the region who are trying to rebuild their lives.

✟**George Butler**
Reportage illustrator

'Look, the virgin shall conceive and bear a son,
    and they shall name him Emmanuel,'
which means, 'God is with us'.

Matthew 1: 23 (NRSV)

According to the sailor Sir Robin Knox-Johnston, 'there is no such thing as an atheist in the Southern Ocean.' When we're truly afraid and alone, faith can give us hope and courage. When we're at our weakest, faith can help us find true strength.

But what about the everyday? Can faith help us then?

My own Christian faith can be difficult to articulate. It's like describing ice cream, or swimming – words will only get you so far. Better to try it for yourself. But what I can say is that my faith tells me that I am known, that I am loved, and that I am forgiven – regardless of how many times I fall and fail.

I've tried to do without it. And I've survived, for a while – but alone we can never be fully empowered. Time and many adventures have taught me that to be complete and fully alive I need this life-giving presence that faith provides. It is almost as if, over time, I have found the courage to admit that my longing for this life of love and faith is stronger than the pride that says we have to do it all alone.

It's a point of awareness. It takes some humility to relinquish control. But it is the starting point of true adventure. Just read some of the great stories of old, if you are in any doubt there.

Some might call faith a crutch. But what does a crutch do? It helps us stand and it gives us a weapon to fight with. I like that analogy! And as time goes on, there's no doubt that I need that strength more and more, every day, to tackle the battles of life and to climb the mountains we all face.

(By the way, faith is different from religion. I mean, I meet a ton of people who don't want 'religion'. I get it. I have always felt the same. So did Jesus. He was the least religious, the most free and probably the wildest character I know of. He loved a party and hung out with the rejected, the untamed and the outsiders. The only people he seems to get angry with were the overly religious hypocrites.)

Faith, though, is a journey. To walk in it in our everyday lives takes courage. All too often it's the tougher path. But life and the wild have taught me that the tougher path almost always ends up being the most fulfilling one.

When it comes to quietly bowing the knee and asking for his presence to bring you peace, strengthen your spirit and lead you into light – well, we have nothing to lose, and everything to gain.

That's grace.

✝Bear Grylls
Global adventurer, bestselling author and Chief Scout

For thirty-seven years I spent my life going to the theatre four or five nights a week, writing reviews to tight deadlines and thinking about little except work. At 59, realising I was completely burnt out, I resigned, and for three heady months enjoyed a sense of freedom and happiness.

Then I woke up one morning feeling the stirrings of the clinical depression I'd experienced several times before. The big questions loomed. *What am I for? What is the point? Gosh, I feel rotten.* My job had become so overwhelming that I didn't know who I was once I stopped. What followed was loneliness, desperation and a plunging pit of despair.

It was suggested I might help move the chairs for Connections, the group my local church runs for seniors. I wasn't very good at that due to my poor spatial awareness. But the warm welcome helped.

When I started attending Connections myself, I found that in talking with the seniors my own feelings of anxiety and despair began to lighten. I discovered that I was quite good at chatting and cheering people up. I began to enjoy the amazing vibe of generations coming together to find comfort in the Church and each other.

I had found it hard to believe in God, but now I became less critical in my views, not least because of the peace and contentment of many at Connections, often in difficult circumstances.

My faith is still far from strong but I never feel closer to God than when I'm enjoying fellowship with the wise good-hearted guests. I will always be grateful to Pippa and Mike for their encouragement and for the sense of purpose and belonging I have found.

The thing I love is the feeling of usefulness in serving others; being free from self and closer to God.

✦**Charlie Spencer**
Retired journalist
Volunteer at Connections, Holy Trinity Church, Claygate

In the beginning was the Word …

Words have formed the basis of human communication, and through the written word that communication can transcend the constraints of distance and time. Words we share with one another articulate our thoughts and feelings, and so the Word, in Jesus, makes God fully known to us – the expression of God himself.

This year through words I have been able to share my relationship with Jesus in my book *Eye Can Write*. Throughout my life I have felt the tangible presence of Jesus with me, sustaining, comforting and guiding me through the rhythms of life. But it was only when I learnt to spell using my eyes on a Perspex alphabet board that I could share my faith.

The following poem is based on a wordless meditation on Christmas night – using words.

✦**Jonathan Bryan**
Author of Eye Can Write
Founder of the charity Teach Us Too

God's Grace

A poem by Jonathan Bryan

Laughter of reunion voices
Fading through the night breeze,
Secluded in obscurity,
Cry of life – born for me.

Exhilarated exhaustion
Carved on Mary's face,
Faintly inklings of foreboding
Echoing loving grace.

Vulnerable humility,
Divine, dependent boy.
Thousand years of prophetic light,
Lavished blessing – our joy.

Running feet, gruff country voices,
Shepherds shyly shuffle,
Angelic announcement sharing,
Lost in awe, most humble.

Shafts of moonlight illuminate,
The sound of peace descends.
Embodied freedom sleeping now,
God's love surrounds, transcends.

As with many things in life, I was first introduced to the fact that Christmas is not always a happy occasion through the profound medium of the BBC drama *EastEnders*. As a child, gathering at my grandmother's house with my Ghanaian family, one auntie or another would always insist on tuning into the long-running soap opera. It usually involved a huge marital row in the pub, or revelations of betrayal, followed by tears, shouting or tragic loneliness. I could never understand why anyone would imagine such misery on what was, to me, such an uncomplicated, happy day.

My blissful ignorance was preserved, I now realise, by the hard work of older family members; sheltering us children in a bubble of conventional Christmas comforts. These included – in place of our usual treat of kenkey and fried fish – a traditional English roast, gifts, chocolate coins, pudding with custard. My grandmother was a devoted Christian, but my parents, my sister and I attended our local Anglican church only once a year, on Christmas Eve, for a magical midnight Mass.

Conventions can ground us, bringing us the spiritual reassurance of ritual and commemoration, or offering stability, comfort and cultural certainty. But this year, I have been reflecting too on the risk that convention can serve to shelter us from our reality, numb us to our humanity, or blind us from the sanctity of life.

The book *Mrs Bridge*, by Evan S. Connell, is a searing example of the danger. It tells of a woman who observes social convention as devotedly as her religion, obeying all the gender and social rules, acting swiftly to eradicate any signs of individuality in her children. Her compassion never stretches to imagining the suffering of others outside her bubble of house staff, dinner parties and country clubs. The result is a deep emptiness she never musters the courage to explore. 'Some people go skimming over the years of existence to sink gently into a placid grave,' Connell observes, 'ignorant of life to the last'.

This resonates all the more for me because my life is becoming more unconventional. I published a book this year revealing some of the already unconventional aspects of my own personal life, and swapped a full-time job for life as an author. These are hard decisions for someone with a young family. But they have brought me closer to my sense of purpose and deepest beliefs than ever before. Emboldening myself to flout convention feels as if it has brought me freedom.

I could have done more to help others, to fight for justice, or to share my resources with those in need. These are my own failings. But convention has helped create an environment in which such failings seem justified, where the status quo is preserved and inequality is normal. At their worst, conventions help us skim over life, forgetting that this is our one chance to leave this world better than we found it.

Conventions can bring joy and reassurance, just like they did to my childhood Christmas. But at this time of year, more than any other, rather than thoughtlessly let conventions select me, I hope to select them; because I've realised they serve love.

✦**Afua Hirsch**
Author, journalist and broadcaster

In the sixth month the angel Gabriel was sent by God to a town in Galilee called Nazareth, to a virgin engaged to a man whose name was Joseph, of the house of David. The virgin's name was Mary. And he came to her and said, 'Greetings, favoured one! The Lord is with you.' But she was much perplexed by his words and pondered what sort of greeting this might be. The angel said to her, 'Do not be afraid, Mary, for you have found favour with God. And now, you will conceive in your womb and bear a son, and you will name him Jesus. He will be great, and will be called the Son of the Most High, and the Lord God will give to him the throne of his ancestor David. He will reign over the house of Jacob for ever, and of his kingdom there will be no end.' Mary said to the angel, 'How can this be, since I am a virgin?' The angel said to her, 'The Holy Spirit will come upon you, and the power of the Most High will overshadow you; therefore the child to be born will be holy; he will be called Son of God. And now, your relative Elizabeth in her old age has also conceived a son; and this is the sixth month for her who was said to be barren. For nothing will be impossible with God.' Then Mary said, 'Here am I, the servant of the Lord; let it be with me according to your word.' Then the angel departed from her.

Luke 1: 26–38 (NRSV)

This has been quite a year for me, full of opportunities, challenges and new horizons. I have had to dig deep on many occasions for that inner strength and belief, and grasp hold of my determination and continue towards my dreams. Sound familiar to anyone?

Over the years, I have found it so important to cherish moments of celebration; the resilience of the human spirit and her story deserve to be recognised and we all need to take a moment to observe the diverse, complex, creative and world-changing nation we are.

This Christmas I will be doing exactly that – celebrating and looking forward in anticipation of the great adventures that lie ahead of us all. Great things can be accomplished when we stand together: we become outward- rather than inward-looking, we see the long-term vision rather than the day-to-day struggle and, most importantly, we create the baton of opportunity to hand to the next generation – and that excites me.

✛Jo Malone CBE
Founder and Creative Director, Jo Loves

The Message version of Matthew 11: 28–30 sums up the heart of Christmas for me: 'Are you tired? Worn out? Burned out on religion? Come to me. Get away with me and you'll recover your life. I'll show you how to take a real rest. Walk with me and work with me – watch how I do it. Learn the unforced rhythms of grace. I won't lay anything heavy or ill-fitting on you. Keep company with me and you'll learn to live freely and lightly.'

How I need to learn the unforced rhythms of grace, rather than clumsily continuing to pound the treadmill of London life, which gets ever faster, especially as Christmas approaches. The pressure to be perfect and conform to social expectations adds still more weight to an already heavy load. The need to step away from the treadmill, to lay down our heavy bags and walk with Jesus at his pace is so great, particularly at Christmas, when we celebrate his life and light coming into the world.

I have had the great privilege of spending some time with the Chemin Neuf Community over the past year. Spending time in Community, being vulnerable and learning to set time aside to walk with Jesus, to simplify life, to take delight in others and to breathe, hear and see again has been a great gift. And for me this is the gift of Christmas – not parties, tinsel and cards, but Jesus, the giver of life, freedom and those unforced rhythms of grace.

✝**Joanna Muirhead**
Lawyer and Member of Community of St Anselm 2015–16

A letter to a child at Christmas

How many stars are there in the universe? Do you know?

Actually, no one is quite sure – but there are about 10 billion galaxies, and about 100 billion stars in a galaxy, so that means there are about 1,000,000,000,000,000,000,000 (that's one billion trillion).

And those are just the ones we know about!

We are like teeny-tiny specks in a gigantic universe.

At night, when you look up at the sky, and you see the stars – do you ever feel small? Too small for God to notice? Or care about?

When God looks down does he even see you?

But did you know?

Before God even made the stars – or anything in the universe – he knew your name and the colour of your eyes.

The Bible says that God sang and danced for joy as he made you.

That if you tried to count how many times he thinks about you it would be like trying to count all the grains of sand on the seashore.

That he knows every day you'll ever live,
hears every whisper hidden in your heart,
holds every tear you ever cried.

Because he just can't stop loving you.

He would move heaven and earth to be near you!

And, one night,
long ago in Bethlehem,
he did just that.

Because you see God doesn't just look down.

He came down.

God himself came down.

How did he come?
With trumpets and flags and big armies?

No.

He came in the quiet,
when no one was looking,
in the dead of night.

Where did he go?
To the important people? To a palace or a castle?

No.

He came
to a poor homeless couple
in a tumbledown stable
on the outskirts of a nothing town.

Shh!
Do you see that little baby sleeping in his mother's arms?

He is God Almighty, Maker of the Stars!

Mary and Joseph named him Jesus 'Emmanuel'
which means, 'God has come to live with us'.

Because, of course, he had.

The King of Heaven,
the great creator of the Universe,
the maker of the stars and all the galaxies
had made himself small
and come down
as a tiny little baby.

But why?

Why did he leave his palace and his throne and step out
of Heaven and come down?

For just one reason.

So he could be with
you.

Because he just can't stop loving you.

✦ **Sally Lloyd-Jones**
New York Times bestselling writer,
and sometimes a performer of her work

Milad has just finished second in Australia for classical bodybuilding. Legs submerged, his large torso hovers over the waters of his baptism as his voice shakes to share his story. Tears roll down his brother Meysam's face as Milad tells their testimony of God's goodness. They are both refugees, both yet to be granted permanent protection. Their futures hang between understandable despair and anticipated deliverance. The scars on their bodies are visible as they pose when competing, and visible as they are lowered into the waters of baptism – scars which seem to speak of what God has brought them through. They both know that being Christians means imprisonment, or worse, if they are sent back to Iran.

Nothing challenges the limits of polite middle-class Christmas sermons like people who are willing to risk martyrdom. Their staring down of death bears witness to God's love, and their conviction to never take life because of God's love, silences domesticated preachers and dogmatic atheists alike. That kind of faith, that kind of love, testifies to a particular kind of God – the God revealed to us at Christmas. The Christmas message is the power seen at Calvary, given to us as a baby.

Meysam and Milad's courage and vulnerability are not a paradox. There is no contradiction. In light of the Incarnation, they bear witness to what God's nonviolent power is like. In the manger, God Almighty is revealed as all-vulnerable. In our crucified and risen Messiah, God Almighty reveals divine power to be beyond all coercion – a deeper dynamic than death and a force stronger than all evil, injustice and sin. To quote Milad, as he talks of the authoritarian religious authorities: 'They taught us God is harsh and cruel. But we've seen Jesus. We know God's power is love.'

✦**Jarrod McKenna**
Pastor
Founder of the Common Grace and
cofounder of First Home Project

The shepherds said to one another, 'Let us go now to Bethlehem and see this thing that has taken place, which the Lord has made known to us.' So they went with haste and found Mary and Joseph, and the child lying in the manger. When they saw this, they made known what had been told them about this child; and all who heard it were amazed at what the shepherds told them. But Mary treasured all these words and pondered them in her heart. The shepherds returned, glorifying and praising God for all they had heard and seen, as it had been told them.

Luke 2: 15–20 (NRSV)

Being invited to contribute to this wonderful book has made me reflect carefully on the past year.

One of the most fantastic memories was the first Fire Cadet Games held at Crystal Palace in August, when fire and rescue services from across the country brought together young people from every background, in very friendly but serious competition. It was great fun and I hope the Fire Cadet Games grow every year.

It has also been one of the most remarkable and challenging years of my life. The impact of the terrible Grenfell fire in London continues to cast a long shadow over our community and my teams. I have seen the best in my people who have striven to provide comfort to the survivors and to the victims' families and loved ones when giving evidence. I have seen every one recounting and reliving the terrible events of 14th June 2017.

I hope you will understand the pride I have felt as I have seen my teams, who worked so amazingly bravely for those who cried for help, now turn their efforts to help deliver justice for those we lost, and those who remain in pain.

✦**Dany Cotton**
London Fire Commissioner

December is the time for candles, spiritual light and a sense of miracle. For some it is the belief that they bring the light of Jesus, even in the darkest of times. For others the miracle of the pure oil sufficient for one day which lasted for eight.

With your permission, I would like to light a candle for every family – Israeli and Palestinian, Jewish, Christian and Muslim – which has lost an immediate family member in a conflict that should have ended long ago. For those who have chosen a path of reconciliation rather than revenge. For those who wake up every day to the challenge of continuing to work for peace, no matter the circumstances. Six hundred bereaved Palestinian and Israeli families, all members of the Parents Circle – Families Forum, understand the need to recognise the humanity in the 'other'. They have paid the highest price and yet continue to foster goodwill and hope for a better future.

Let us light a candle for Christine; beloved 12-year-old daughter of Najwa and George, a Christian family from

Bethlehem, who lost her. Let us light another for Roni, who lives in Tel-Aviv and lost his two sons; he works every day to spread a message of reconciliation even though the hole in his generous heart will never heal. Let us light yet another candle for Rami from Jerusalem, whose beautiful daughter was killed in a suicide bombing; he never stops trying to spread a message of understanding. Let us light one for Bassam from Jerusalem, who chose, after seven years in jail, a path of non-violence and dignity even when he lost his beloved daughter.

I could tell you stories of extraordinary people who know that we must stop the violence and the occupation otherwise we will have to share this holy land with graves.

Lastly, I will light a candle for my David. Not a day goes by without remembering his spirit of compassion in my quest for reconciliation and quiet.

✦**Robi Damelin**
Spokesperson and member of the Parents Circle
– Families Forum

The late Dr Howard Thurman was one of the quiet unsung heroes of history. An African American raised in the segregated South of the early twentieth century, he grew up with the indignity of racial separation and injustice. But like many others, he was profoundly influenced by a grandmother who believed in God, and who followed the way of love that Jesus taught and embodied. As a result young Thurman grew into an adult passionately committed to this way of Jesus.

He became a noted preacher and teacher who founded a multiracial church in San Francisco before America had begun to learn the way of racial equality. He taught in seminaries and universities. His influence reached far and wide. Civil rights leaders consulted him quietly and regularly as the spiritual director of the movement.

He is one of the people credited with helping Dr Martin Luther King grasp and embrace the teachings and methodology of Mahatma Gandhi. Dr Thurman's seminal book, *Jesus and the Disinherited*, was so influential for Dr King that he carried it wherever he travelled until the day he died.

A poem that Thurman composed focuses my imagination on the implications of the message of the birth of Jesus.

When the song of the angels is stilled,
When the star in the sky is gone,
When the kings and princes are home,
When the shepherds are back with their flock,
The work of Christmas begins:
To find the lost,
To heal the broken,
To feed the hungry,
To release the prisoner,
To rebuild the nations,
To bring peace among others,
To make music in the heart.

Howard Thurman was right! The work of Christmas is indeed to make music in the heart by making a difference in the lives of others. May you and I make such music this Christmas!

✝**The Most Revd Michael B. Curry**
Presiding Bishop of the Episcopal Church USA

There is strong evidence to suggest physical isolation is the most important factor associated with loneliness. This can be particularly acute for older people living alone, who may struggle with bereavement, ill health, poor mobility, loss of independence, dementia, or just through the exhaustion of caring for a frail partner. Many just need a caring person to sit with them, to listen, and maybe to pray.

As an occupational therapist, I have been aware of these struggles and have longed to provide a safe, welcoming place for elderly church members, and others, who may be lonely and isolated.

Eight years on, Connections is one of the largest weekly gatherings for seniors in the UK. It provides a safe place where guests can experience the love of Jesus. It has grown into a self-supporting community of help and friendship, as well as providing a bridge into church and meeting God.

To help seniors experience the love of God, Connections emphasises:

Welcome: being welcomed warmly is vital. People know they matter, they are known, and they are loved.

Listening: starts where the person is. Someone remembering your recent operation, or the anniversary of your husband dying, shows you matter and are valued. Trust is then built over time.

Generosity: flows from God's grace to us. From coffee and delicious cakes to the incredible support given by the team, Connections seeks to share God's generosity.

Prayer: surrounds and underpins each Connections gathering.

At Archbishop Justin's suggestion and with his encouragement, we have been sharing with many others how similar gatherings can be set up in all sorts of different churches and settings.

My prayer is that others with a heart for older people will ask God how to reach them in their local communities or churches, and that more and more elderly people will discover how amazing God is and the difference he can make to their lives – not only at Christmas, but all year round.

✦**Pippa Cramer**
Pastoral Care and Seniors Minister,
Holy Trinity Church, Claygate

I've always enjoyed celebrating Christmas.

On the council estate where I grew up in south London, its arrival was marked every year by a real buzz and sense of excitement and community spirit. Christmas is a time to celebrate and reflect on the story of the nativity and the birth of Jesus. It's also an opportunity for us to come together and spend precious time with our families, friends and loved ones. Together, we look back at the year that has passed, and as the new year comes into view, look forward with renewed hope.

Whether it's donating to charity, caring for the sick and the vulnerable, or feeding the homeless at Christmas, it's clear that Christian values of love, compassion and generosity have enhanced our society and made our city and country a better place. As Mayor of London I'm determined to shine a light on the huge contribution made by our Christian community and to promote London as a place that is open and welcoming to all faiths.

At this special time of year, I'd like to wish you a joyful Christmas.

✛**The Rt. Hon. Sadiq Khan**
Mayor of London

My name is Dorothy and I shall be 90 years old on 29th December this year. I have lived in Claygate, Surrey, since 1957 and have three children, six grandchildren and one great-grandson.

I had a wonderful marriage to Tom for sixty-three years until his death in 2015. He had been ill for some time but his last wish was to be at home and I had the privilege of helping him through his final days. When told the doctors could do no more, he asked me and the children, 'Who will look after Mum?' and I found myself saying, 'God will look after me.' We held hands and prayed the Lord's Prayer together.

Losing Tom was hard and painful. Grief and loneliness are not easy. But my son Stephen contacted Pippa at our local church, who then visited me and invited me to Connections, their weekly gathering of seniors.

I have been coming ever since! It has been so helpful to meet people in similar situations and to be part of a community again. Connections has helped connect me with new and old friends, and I feel more connected to God too.

It has taken me on a journey, getting to know God. I attended a short series of sessions called *Hymns We Love*, where we sang familiar hymns and talked about what the words meant. Following this, I was confirmed at a special service at church and then Pippa and I were invited by Archbishop Justin to a carol service at Lambeth Palace! I am a very ordinary lady but I feel God has been very kind to me.

As I approach my eighty-ninth Christmas, I am so thankful to God for the support and love of not just my family, but my new extended church family.

I encourage anyone who has elderly relatives or neighbours to remember how much they appreciate seeing you and being involved with your Christmas plans. I also wish that other churches could hold Connections-style gatherings, as you cannot overestimate the difference that kindness and care can make to someone like me.

✝**Dorothy Horn**
Guest at Connections, Holy Trinity Church, Claygate

Jesus declared: 'I am the bread that came down from heaven' (John 6: 41 NRSV).

I bring you glad tidings from the city of the nativity, Bethlehem – a city which today, like much of the world, hungers for peace and justice. Bethlehem in Aramaic means 'the house of bread' and the name of the city is incredibly fitting, given its location as the birthplace of he that is the Bread of Heaven.

Jesus' birth narratives, as we find them in the Gospels of Luke and Matthew, are full of imagery and symbolism. These images which the Evangelists illuminate reflect deep meaning and shine light upon the historic events of the nativity, a light which permeates the whole of human life and across the entirety of creation.

Here, I want to focus on the image of the stable where Jesus was born. In Luke's Gospel, we find that Jesus was laid by his mother Mary in a manger, a place where animals are fed. Jesus was born in a manger to be the spiritual food for the whole of creation. Through his birth, Christ, clothed in humanity, became the manna that descended from heaven so that the world may be nourished by his own life-giving bread. Jesus' incarnation as the Son of God in human flesh was for the sake of the salvation of the whole world. The Incarnation of the Son of God shone light and brought life for all.

Today we live in a world that hungers for so many things: peace and reconciliation; food and water; economic and social stability; safety and security; independence and liberation; healing of broken relationships. This is a list and litany that can go on and on. Christmas is a time when we remember the offerings of the shepherds and the Magi to the Christ child, and in response, offer our small gifts to our hungry world. We as Christians are fed by the bread of Jesus in order to feed and nourish others.

Our bidding prayer for this Christmas season is to remember, through our loving action, all those who hunger for a life filled with human dignity. May the Babe of Bethlehem be our daily bread where all are nourished, in the glory of God the Father, and in the power of the Holy Spirit. Amen.

✟**The Very Revd Canon Hosam Naoum**
Dean of St George's Cathedral, Jerusalem

A small miracle happened in my life a while ago.

As a mother and mediator, I am acutely aware how often we are defined by divisions and distinctions even within families, and I'm accustomed to this usual order of things.

Over a year ago, I visited a carol service within a prison. I was surrounded by other visitors and many residents, all of us a diverse bunch at every age and stage, career and culture.

A small gospel choir of four elderly ladies began to sing. As the singing embraced us, I felt something begin to connect each of us. A joy was ignited across the room.

As we heard the familiar Christmas readings, and people told their own stories, a remarkable thing began to happen. I noticed that I was no longer caught up by being a 'visitor in a prison'; my identity seemed no longer to be defined by culture, class, aspiration or failure, who and what I was or who anyone else was. The same appeared to be happening for everyone.

We had become fellow guests – distinctions and divisions dissolved, absorbed by a new focus and that small miracle of unity.

I then recognised that a similar thing had happened two days before this.

I had been a visitor to a palace and the occasion was another carol service. There I had recognised quite a few from TV, film and the media, and it had been a hugely exciting moment to be among a few stars! Yet as people shared stories and readings, an identical transformation had taken place.

We heard from a refugee; then from another living in a homeless shelter; then from an elderly lady for whom life had become bleak as loneliness set in following the death of her husband.

Each told us how the care and the help of individuals and strangers had made all the difference.

I found my focus had become absorbed by the miracle of kindness, by the surprise of hope. And status, stardom and the 'I' had lost their glitter; the normal order dissolved.

We were joyously and simply fellow guests: each invited, uniquely welcomed.

So this took place in a palace, the same wonder reoccurred in a prison and I guess two thousand years ago, the visitors (some kings and some shepherds) found that they too became fellow guests before a manger in a stable.

✦**Fiona Ruttle**
Wife and mother, artist, mediator, kayaker

In her Christmas message, the Queen rightly pays tribute to our armed forces, especially those on duty and away from their families during this time. It's a poignant year for the military as we look back to mark the 100th anniversary of the First World War, giving thanks for the sacrifices made, and as we look forward by modernising our defence posture to deal with a fast-changing and ever more complex world.

Although the challenges we face today are different, what remains unchanged from 100 years ago is the character of our soldiers, sailors and air personnel. Their leadership, teamwork, discipline, grit and tenacity are what make them the most professional armed forces in the world.

We owe an enormous debt of gratitude to all who serve and have served. They not only stand in harm's way but help underline our values and our global reputation. The majority are able to depart the armed forces and utilise their skills as civilians. A small minority, through no fault of their own, may spend this Christmas alone, homeless or dealing with challenges relating to their service. Some 400 invaluable service-facing charities do an incredible job providing vital help and expertise for our veteran community.

Let us all help raise spirits this Christmas by simply saying a big 'thank you' to our armed forces personnel and valiant veterans for their service to our country.

✝**The Rt. Hon. Tobias Ellwood**
Member of Parliament for Bournemouth East
Minister for Defence People and Veterans

with a twinkle in his eye and three cameras round his neck. We ate hot curries with our fingers sitting cross-legged on the deck, and I learned that for him the camera was a powerful instrument of social change. That conversation has continued over the intervening years, in the roadside tea stalls of the subcontinent and at the conference tables of Europe. The common ground between us, the joint belief in justice, transcend the ordinary boundaries of our lives.

During a recent televised interview, Shahidul criticised his government. He was measured but firm, as is his way. Two hours later he was beaten up by plainclothes police, imprisoned and tortured. The Government said he had been spreading false propaganda and inciting unrest.

This is an easy excuse to get rid of opposition. Pontius Pilate realised that. Christ's teachings, his championing of the dispossessed, and his willingness to die for his beliefs — these were the real threat. Pontius declined to stick his neck out.

My wife Jan and I were in Transylvania last year when a godson called from England. He had broken his neck in a rugby match. The nurse was holding his phone and he was about to be wheeled into the operating theatre. The prognosis was bad. Would Jan pray for him? She did. Priests and friends were electronically rustled up across the world, and they did too. He is back teaching teenagers in Toxteth. The surgeon said it was a miracle.

When the news about Shahidul came through I enlisted Jan's support again. Prayers were said in churches and cathedrals from Liverpool to Nairobi, from Shrewsbury to Mexico. Shahidul is still incarcerated, but he is alive. In a country where the disappeared tend to stay disappeared, this too is a miracle.

Martyrs bear witness to the truth for which they die. Their deaths announce the ultimate inviolability of that truth. As Dr Martin Luther King observed, 'the man who won't die for something isn't fit to live.' Shahidul does deserve to live. I shall pray for his life and freedom this Christmas, for he is a beacon of light in a darkening world.

✦**Rupert Grey**
Lawyer, traveller, photographer and carpenter

Seventeen years ago Billy walked through the doors of our church. He was 32 stone (448 lbs) and could barely walk. He had a thick Glaswegian accent and a fuse that was extremely short. He would fly off the handle and rant at any perceived slight, waving his walking sticks around as he bellowed at anyone who disagreed with him and regularly walking out, vowing at least three or four times per year never to return.

With great trepidation we agreed to try to support him through a charity at our church called Caring for Ex-Offenders. With the help of his support team – social workers, doctors and two wonderful and very patient police officers named Steve and Jason – we looked at how to get him involved, while ensuring the safety of the congregation and the public.

You see, Billy had come directly from Barlinnie Prison, having served thirty-seven years at Her Majesty's pleasure, split between prison and psychiatric hospital. Nobody was entirely sure how he would cope with being released. He had had both a lobotomy and brain damage, caused by a hammer blow shortly before his arrest (across his head was a terrifying scar). Nobody was completely certain which had caused more damage, but his mental capacity was around that of an eight year old, and so was his emotional age – all presented in a very big and intimidating body. It was apparent that he was always going to need a lot of support.

None of this boded well for us, and we were (to be blunt) very anxious. I became Billy's mentor with my husband Karl, who was always referred to by Billy as 'the Boss'.

Billy joined our midweek group, immediately declaring himself responsible for welcoming guests at Sunday services. He would terrify them with his toothless grin, and enthusiastically insist that they sit right in the front row, while interrogating them to make sure that they weren't drunk.

None of this sounds very positive but I am certain now that Billy has had more of an impact on our church than almost any other member.

Billy died in his sleep at home in March, after an illness that had eventually resulted in the amputation of his foot. A week earlier we had celebrated his seventieth birthday – more than twenty of us squeezed into one booth in a coffee shop in the hospital, Billy beaming with joy and pride and calling over any passing medical staff to meet his friends and family.

At his memorial service it was standing room only. I was overwhelmed by the number of people who wanted to speak about how spending time with Billy had transformed them and their lives.

That word *family* came to mean something very different through spending time with Billy; *inclusive* gained a new reality after accepting someone who the world – quite reasonably – had decided should never be accepted; who had offended in a way that meant most people would feel valid in declaring him an outcast.

We learned to be patient, to slow down. To value relationships and friendships for the person and not for what they could offer to us. To value loyalty. To get over any tendency to present the outwardly perfect as the bar to aim for. To think about how we really could include everyone. This Christmas Day more than 400 people will gather for a five-course dinner that started when we realised that Christmas was a very lonely time for a man who wasn't allowed into family homes. We decided to start and host a lunch at the church for him and others who would otherwise be alone. It grew and grew.

Christmas this year will be a quieter affair, but we will miss Billy and his ability to make us reflect on everything through very different eyes.

✦The Revd Jo Davies
Anglican Chaplain at Her Majesty's Prison, Pentonville

Due to my job I've lived in a few different countries, and I've spent Christmas in four of them. Each year at Christmas time, I reflect on the similarities and differences across those countries and consider what we're celebrating.

In my home country of Argentina, Christmas is not very commercial. As with all countries in the southern hemisphere, Christmas occurs in the summer. Many people celebrate by going to church and having dinner at home. At midnight, nearly everyone celebrates by lighting fireworks and going out with friends. It doesn't feel religious; it is a tradition of partying with friends on a quasi-religious pretext.

In the United States (and to a lesser extent in England and Canada), I feel Christmas is treated differently. Everything seems to revolve around the coming holiday. There are entire radio stations devoted to Christmas music; TV episodes 'celebrating' the season; along with movies, toys, outfits, home decorations, and so on. It feels that during December, people only care about having time off and celebrating with family. Despite the constant focus on Christmas, it feels like it is not about Christ.

Irrespective of where I am in the world, I go to Christmas Mass and I always have the same feeling. Some people are there because they believe, some because it is a family tradition, some because they want to reconnect with the church, and some because they are curious. I love seeing how welcoming all Christian churches are during those days, but in my mind, faith in God isn't just about attendance at church. Rather, true faith is transformative and shapes how we act in the world. In that light, I always try to remember Isaiah 1: 16–17, where the prophet lists practical actions for a faithful life.

How much better would we be as a society if all of us who attended church (at Christmas or during the year) dedicated ourselves in ways big and small to seeking justice and defending the vulnerable?

I've seen many differences in how Christmas is celebrated across the world, but there are commonalities as well. For me, Christmas is the recognition that Jesus came among us and fundamentally changed the world. When people come to church, I pray that hearts – including mine – will be transformed so that all can become good, free of judgement, with servant hearts, tirelessly defending the weak and pursuing justice. In short, to become more like Jesus!

✝**Ignacio Fantaguzzi**
Strategy Consultant
Member of the Community of St Anselm

*But when the fullness of time had come, God sent his
Son, born of a woman, born under the law, in order
to redeem those who were under the law, so that we
might receive adoption as children. And because you
are children, God has sent the Spirit of his Son into our
hearts, crying, 'Abba! Father!' So you are no longer a slave
but a child, and if a child then also an heir, through God.*

Galatians 4: 4–7 (NRSV)

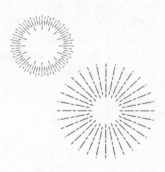

I am a storyteller.

Ever since I was a child, I have been drawn to stories, folk tales, books, words, the letters of the alphabet. Always a nomad, I have left traces of my past in this city and that, like a cardigan that has snagged on rogue nails along the way. I guess I am used to the idea of 'portable homelands'. My motherland is Storyland. That's where I feel most at home. Being a novelist is a lonely art. Paradoxically, by retreating into the solitude of literature, I feel like I can connect with humanity, past and present.

But as much as I am in love with stories, I am equally interested in silences – the things we cannot talk about, the taboos. There is a part of me that wants to bring the periphery to the centre; give more power to the disempowered and connect with the Other. To insist on the act of remembering in the face of collective, forceful amnesia.

I come from Turkey – a country of collective amnesia. Where the complexities of history are denied through a filter of ultra-nationalism and jingoism. Where 'official history' is always his-story. In my novels I like to ask, 'Where were the women, where were the minorities, where were the poor ... where were the Others who are not included in official history? What were their stories like?'

All extremist ideologies aim to dehumanise the Other. If they can manage to do that, they can do anything afterwards. Racism, sexism, ultra-nationalism, and xenophobia ... it is not a coincidence that they all portray the Other as less human. But the art of storytelling does the opposite. Stories re-humanise those who have been dehumanised; connect us through invisible threads of understanding and empathy. In the world of literature there is no us and them. The Other is no other than me.

Yet we live in a world that systematically denies us our right to be complex. Nuances are not welcome anymore. On TV, radio and the internet, it has become the norm to bring together two angry speakers with opposite views and make them clash. If they shout at each other, all the better for the ratings. Even in academia, where nuanced thinking should find a warm welcome, most of the debates are reduced to either–or dichotomies. Are you one of us, or are you one of them? We are being pushed into antagonistic identities and narrow tribes of the like-minded. It reminds me of Rumi's lines: 'You were born with wings, why prefer to crawl?'

We human beings contain multitudes inside. Why do we prefer to be reduced to uniform tribes?

I do not have a single identity based on race, ethnicity, or ideology. I have multiple belongings; an Istanbulite just like the poet Cavafy, who said, 'This city will follow me wherever I go, so deep is my love and longing for Istanbul'. There are many elements in my soul from the Middle East, and the East; the Aegean Sea and the Balkans. And I embrace them all with respect. I am a European by birth and the core values that I uphold. I am a Londoner, profoundly attached to this beautiful city … I'd like to think of myself as a mixture of East and West. A global soul in our fascinating planet Earth.

Why accept being reduced to an imaginary tribe? Swim against the tide, though the tide is strong and it might get worse. To fight for humanism and dignity for all – regardless of race, gender or class – is to fight for multiplicity. Fight for humankind.

✦**Elif Shafak**
Author, storyteller, women's rights activist

This Advent I'm reflecting on choice.

God's incredible choice to send his Son to die for us. Christ's choice to lovingly meet those despised and rejected by society. The choice we get to make everyday: to love our neighbours, friends and enemies.

One of the choices we most neglect to talk about, I feel, is the choice to love ourselves. In Matthew 22: 39 (NRSV), Jesus said, 'You shall love your neighbour as yourself.' While we're called to love others, we are also called to love ourselves. We are called to choose ourselves.

Loving others and loving yourself are two sides of the same coin, intended to be in perfect balance. Destroying yourself by putting everyone else's needs ahead of yours only creates suffering – yours. Destroying those around you by being selfish only creates suffering – theirs.

Choose to love yourself this Advent by saying no to the commitments that are too much, to the family members who are toxic or to the friends who don't value you. Choose to love yourself by saying yes to new experiences, yes to people who uplift you, yes to what you really want.

Although I do not know whose dinner table I'll be sitting at come Christmas Day, what I do know is that wherever I am will be somewhere I've chosen through a love for myself and the other people at the table. If that's not a blessing, I don't know what is.

✦**Ellis Jones**
Member of the Youthscape community

Greetings from Bethlehem,

Another year is soon coming to an end; a year full of wars, fear, hopelessness, despair and darkness. A brother is against his brother, a nation is against another nation and people are killing each other in the name of their religions. In Palestine, we are still living under occupation and our situation is getting worse. Justice and peace are so far from us. Is there still any hope for our broken world?

The prophet Isaiah writes: 'The people who walked in darkness have seen a great light; those who lived in a land of deep darkness – on them a light has shined' (Isaiah 9: 2 NRSV).

In this dark time that our world is going through, the words are still talking to us. God is sending a Saviour, his name is Emmanuel, 'God is with us'. With the birth of Jesus Christ, the prophecy of Isaiah was fulfilled – God reconciled with the broken world through his Son, the light of the world.

Today, we feel that we are in a dark tunnel without a way out. But we should always remember that the candle of hope is still burning, and its light will overcome the deep darkness of our world.

With the end of this year, we complete twenty-eight years of a legal battle in the Israeli courts – trying to protect our farm from the danger of confiscation – without getting tired. We will continue our struggle for justice following a different path; a nonviolent and a creative way of resistance, overcoming evil with good, darkness with light, hatred with love, under our slogan, 'We refuse to be enemies'.

The message of Tent of Nations for the coming year is to continue working on transforming hopelessness, frustration, pain and fear into a positive power that can make a difference.

We wish you happy celebrations and a wonderful new year; a year full of hope, love and fulfilment of your dreams.

We ask God to renew our strength for this coming year, to carry on and continue to work for justice and to be witnesses for this light to all people.

Blessings and Salaam from the city where the Word became flesh.

✝ **Daoud Nassar**
Director, Tent of Nations

Christmas is traditionally a time to give thanks, to reflect on the year gone by and to look forward to the year ahead. How will I measure if my year has been well spent? And what will I give thanks for this festive season? As Christmas approaches, I look back on what has been an extraordinary year; a year that has been full of firsts and has sometimes taken me far outside my comfort zone.

This year I am thankful to be in the privileged position of working alongside a quite incredible young man. This young man has achieved more in his twelve years than most do in a lifetime and yet he was never expected to 'achieve' very much at all. It was deemed impossible that he would walk or talk, and unlikely that he would even recognise his own parents. And now, with a published book under his belt and a charity, Teach Us Too, established in the name of his strong conviction that all children should be taught to read and write regardless of their labels, Jonathan Bryan has certainly 'achieved'.

As his home tutor and now a charity trustee, I have been honoured to accompany Jonathan on his journey to finding his 'voice'. Nonverbal and quadriplegic, Jonathan communicates using his eyes to point, selecting letter by letter what he wants to 'say' and write on a Perspex alphabet board. With his 'voice' unlocked and flying free, he is using his precious earthly time to fight for the rights of others like him. He yearns for them to feel the joy of independently telling their loved ones exactly how they feel; to get pleasure becoming lost in the pages of a book, or giving life to the words in their imagination.

If even one child has been impacted, one teacher inspired, or one parent given hope by the work of Teach Us Too, I will consider this a year well spent.

For the grace of God has appeared, bringing salvation to all, training us to renounce impiety and worldly passions, and in the present age to live lives that are self-controlled, upright, and godly, while we wait for the blessed hope and the manifestation of the glory of our great God and Saviour, Jesus Christ.

Titus 2: 11–13 (NRSV)

In many households, expectations around Christmas are high. Not in mine.

'When will Dad be ill?' is a fairly frequent comment from the children, who are used to the fact that by Christmas Day vicars get to the point where they run out of resistance to any disease going. Or, 'So what's going to be the drama this year?'

It always seems that there is some sort of drama.

There was the year of the dog. Bramble and I went for a run in the local woods at 6.30 p.m. on Christmas Eve: she smelt something interesting, disappeared and did not come back. The atmosphere in the house during the day was one of deep depression. Christmas was ruined. Thirteen long hours later I was standing on an open-top bus in front of five thousand people (one of Canterbury's great Christmas gatherings); my phone buzzed and – very rudely, but I promise unusually – I answered. Bramble had been found; Christmas was saved and I, and the head of the cathedral, jumped up and down for joy.

There was the year of pneumonia. Feverish coughing and feeling generally awful, I had to cancel preaching in Canterbury Cathedral on Christmas Day. Unusually, the diagnosis of pneumonia was a huge relief – 36 hours before I had been visiting an Ebola clinic in Sierra Leone. I remember looking up at a fairly surprised GP and a rather concerned family. But, the precautions that wonderful clinic took meant I was much luckier than those I had visited. I quickly recovered.

It is quite easy to assume that Christmas is to be survived, rather than enjoyed. But I am not in the least cynical, because every year there is something, as I look back over the previous twelve months, which speaks to me of the miracle of God coming to be with us.

Let's be clear. Christmas is not really about babies and mangers. Jesus is Emmanuel – God with us. God came to live among us; to be born and live and have his flesh crucified by others, all so he could be with us. There is nothing human God does not understand or, in Jesus, does not witness. He flipped our understanding of power on its head, arriving as a newborn baby with no protection, no army and none of the gaudy trappings of power.

As is common to all our lives, this year has had great highs and lows. As my wife Caroline and I continue our travels across the Anglican Communion, we spend time with Christians in utterly different circumstances to our own; often, circumstances of war and profound hardship. My hope always, in visiting others, is to offer companionship and witness; to show that, no matter the darkness that has descended, they are not forgotten.

A high point of my year was, of course, the Royal Wedding; an extraordinary day which felt both personal and global. Bishop Michael Curry proclaimed the glad tidings of the revolutionary power of the love of God. His words ringing out in the Chapel, as we celebrated God's love in such spectacular fashion, are a memory I will treasure.

In places of suffering, and places of wealth and privilege, Jesus is present to us all; present as the one who loves us until death and beyond. As I celebrate Christmas this year, listen to the readings and carols, I will pray to receive and be a witness to the revolution of love that arrived as God becoming a vulnerable baby.

✝**The Most Revd Justin Welby**
Archbishop of Canterbury

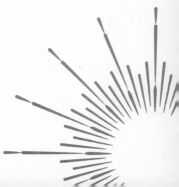

A Closing Prayer

Heavenly Father,

At Christmas your light shone.

Your light shone with searching, loving, penetrating, illuminating, beautiful brilliance.

Even when they tried to extinguish Him your light could not be overcome.

Come again to us in the midst of all that surrounds us, that we may live in your light, so we might share that light with others.

Amen.

An Introduction to our Authors

In the nearly six years since his enthronement, Archbishop Justin has travelled to each of the thirty-nine global provinces of the Anglican Communion. He has met, spoken and prayed with people in parishes, prisons, refugee camps and in governments; at summits, state banquets and gatherings of every description.

We could never do justice to the full wonder of these encounters in one book, but through these assembled messages, we hope to provide a window through which you can glimpse the Archbishop's ministry.

Most importantly, our hope is that you may be as enriched by these messages as the Archbishop has been by their authors.

By way of introduction to each author, the following pages include the biographies they have shared, together with a little explanation of how they came to know Archbishop Justin. Many of them have passed through the doors here at Lambeth Palace; but the community of which they have become an integral part has no physical roots – nor any geographical bounds. The Palace affords a beautiful setting in which to welcome and share in celebration and worship. However it is in communion that community has its permanent home.

Dr Agnes Abuom
Moderator for the World Council of Churches Central
Committee.

✦

*"Sisters all over the world, there is no excuse for your violations.
You should never accept violence against women as the norm.
Whether as a weapon of war ... or in the home, parish or
society. There is no excuse for sexual or gender-based violence.
No excuse. No excuse. No excuse."*

*Ending violence against women is one of the many issues –
including conflict, poverty and racial and structural injustices
– which drive Agnes' extraordinary work and activism.*

*A member of the Anglican Church in Kenya, Agnes is
the Moderator for the World Council of Churches Central
Committee – an assembly of all Christian denominations. So
significant have her contributions been to ecumenism, that in
2017 Archbishop Justin was thrilled to award her the Lambeth
Cross for Ecumenism.*

*It is not possible to adequately measure the effects of violence,
conflict and war, so it is equally impossible to measure the efforts
to end them. But what we can be sure of is that, without the
work of people like Agnes, so many would feel the difference.*

Benjamin
A refugee who fled persecution in Iran, Benjamin is a member
of the Church of England and the British community.

✦

*Anxious to hear more about the Church's work to welcome
and support those arriving in our country, Archbishop Justin*

invited a group of Iranian refugees to Lambeth Palace.

As Christians, they had each faced the same terrible choice: stay put and risk that the threats were empty; or flee and begin a life elsewhere. One among them had walked two thousand miles to reach safety. Another was Benjamin.

Since this first meeting with Archbishop Justin a few years ago, Benjamin has not only become a friend to Lambeth Palace but a member – a precious addition – of the Church of England. It is tricky to write freely of all that Benjamin has brought to our community, as he must remain anonymous and his relocation is no guarantee of safety. Particularly, as his family who – still in Iran – could so easily be targeted for Benjamin's crimes: being a Christian and leaving the country.

Matt Brittin

Matt is President at Google Europe, leading business and operations in Europe, the Middle East and Africa, helping consumers and businesses make the most of digital opportunities. He serves on the boards of Sainsbury's and the Media Trust charity. Previously he worked in the newspaper industry, at McKinsey & Co. consulting, and in real estate, having graduated from the University of Cambridge.

✦

Archbishop Justin was thrilled when Google invited him to their London offices to be part of their speakers' programme, where he was brilliantly interviewed by Matt and questioned by Google staff. The discussion ranged from censorship to the British economy; from the Gospel to Google's future.

The visit left a real impression on the Archbishop. It is clear that Matt and his team have an insatiable desire to engage with ideas; an energy that fuels an eternal quest to reimagine how we might think, communicate and process information. Yet this buzz of creativity is tempered by the enormous responsibility of being a global tech firm. They are faced with the increasingly complex challenge of preserving freedom of speech and access to information, while impeding those with malicious intent.

Of course, Google recognise their role in this and are not perfect (we discussed that too), but the relentless maze of issues created by our existence online is not just for the tech giants to confront. We each need to join the conversation in addressing what is perhaps the greatest challenge of the century: how to manage the internet – a conversation Archbishop Justin hopes very much to continue.

Jonathan Bryan

Campaigner for all children to be taught to read and write regardless of their label. Founder of the charity Teach Us Too; author of *Eye Can Write: A Memoir of a Child's Silent Soul Emerging*.

✦

When Chantal Bryan was pregnant with Jonathan she was in a terrible accident. As a result, Jonathan was born with many health issues, unable to do more than flick his eyes and smile. He would never be able to speak or read – in the conventional way.

Twelve years on and Jonathan is a published author: the result of his own determination and the dedication of his teacher Sarah, his mother Chantal and the rest of his wonderful family. They all came to Lambeth Palace a few months ago to spend time with Archbishop Justin. We watched as Sarah held up the alphabet board for Jonathan; he flicked his eyes across the board *and, as Sarah pointed to the letters, Chantal spoke his words. The process was simple yet astonishing to watch.*

Archbishop Justin and the Bryans talked of many things: the struggles of changing our country's perception of children facing similar challenges; the goodness of Jesus and his promise waiting for us after this life on earth; and how Jonathan is trying to prepare his sisters for life without him.

Well, some talked … Bored of the Archbishop and their big brother, Jemima and Susannah went exploring. They returned clutching treasures found in Archbishop Justin's study, curious about what they were.

"Ah, they are beautiful, aren't they. Well found. They were given to me by Pope Francis."

"Oh," the girls replied, "who's he?"

George Butler

George Butler is an award-winning reportage artist and illustrator. His work, done *in situ* in pen and ink has taken him to places all over the world – including most recently Iraq and Syria. He has been published widely including by The Guardian, The Times and the BBC. He has had several exhibitions of his work including at Lambeth Palace and the Bankside Gallery. In 2014 he set up the Hands Up Foundation with three friends, which so far has raised £3.5 million for projects in Syria.

✦

George is a young artist, an illustrator who chronicles our world through drawings in pen, ink and watercolour. George's travels have taken him down gold mines, up oil rigs, into international law courts and across borders (largely on foot it seems) to Syria,

Gaza, Mosul and more. As he says: "the skill is to use drawing as an interview technique for an entire situation, I make visual notes in ink as time passes. It isn't all about conflict … the drawings are of more common experiences than those on our front pages; they are of unfolding scenes, of habits, of stories, or of a single character."

The Atrium, outside the Crypt Chapel at Lambeth Palace, was home to George's remarkable exhibition earlier this year. For a few months Archbishop Justin's friends and guests could be found captivated by these scenes (often when they were due in meetings upstairs).

Father Raniero Cantalamessa

Born in 1934, Father Raniero Cantalamessa is an Italian Catholic Franciscan priest. Formerly a professor of the History of Ancient Christianity at the Catholic University of Milan, he was appointed Preacher to the Papal Household by John Paul II and reconfirmed by Benedict XVI and Pope Francis. Since 1980, he has preached a weekly sermon during Advent and Lent in the presence of the Pope and the Roman Curia; he is often invited to preach by Christians of other denominations.

✦

For thirty-eight years Father Raniero has been preaching to the Pope and the Roman Curia as the official Preacher to the Papal Household.

Luckily it is not just the Pope who has benefitted from his words and wisdom. Father Raniero's spectacular sermons and writings, gently delivered, have been a source of guidance and energy to millions.

To Archbishop Justin's delight, Father Raniero accepted his invitation in 2015 to address the inaugural service of the Tenth General Synod. Held at Westminster Abbey, the service was a wonderful symbol of Christian unity – a Roman Catholic preaching the Gospel at the heart of the Church of England, with its head, Her Majesty the Queen, in the congregation.

Father Raniero is a remarkable man to whom it is almost impossible to listen without a smile.

Luke Carson

Luke is part of a chaplaincy team in a London prison and works for London City Mission, supporting the street population and mentoring ex-offenders.

✦

Too many people face prison, homelessness and addiction; so often alone. Luke works with the London City Mission to support those facing such issues. He mentors ex-offenders, supports people through drug and alcohol recovery, works at a drop-in centre for the homeless and – for two days a week – joins the chaplaincy team at Pentonville Prison.

Last year, Archbishop Justin invited Luke, and others who support prisoners and mentor ex-offenders, to join him for breakfast and Morning Prayer, keen to hear how he and the Church could better support them.

Luke and his colleagues have since returned to Lambeth Palace for supper and Bible studies with Archbishop Justin and the team, most recently joined by some of their mentees: Mike, Paul, Asaf and a friend. Understandably, palatial corridors lined with enormous portraits can be overwhelming when home has been the inside of a prison cell. But after a calming walk in the garden and as we each settled in, it grew into a lovely evening: the beginning of Archbishop Justin becoming a 'godparent mentor', supporting both mentors and their mentees as often as he can.

The team at Charis Tiwala

Charis Tiwala is a charity that supports people emotionally, practically and spiritually who have been exploited or affected by the sex industry.

✦

Archbishop Justin wanted to visit Charis Tiwala as soon as he heard of it. Since this first meeting in 2015, the Charis team have been regular visitors to Lambeth Palace and have become an essential and much-loved part of our community.

The daily challenge for Charis is to support those affected by the ever-growing sex industry in local brothels, on the street and online. They engage with women in their local area who have been affected or exploited by this industry. They accompany women to various appointments, help with any paperwork and maintain regular contact with relevant police units to ensure the best possible support for those they work with.

With hardly any budget, Charis Tiwala offers a place to talk, cups of tea, card games, baking courses, Bible studies, practical advice and – above all – friendship. The team welcomes those who have nowhere else to feel safe and cared for, unconditionally. Archbishop Justin is amazed by the quiet dedication of the team, and hopes to do justice to the honour of being their patron.

Shane Claiborne

Shane Claiborne is a prominent speaker, activist and best-selling author. He worked with Mother Teresa in Calcutta and founded The Simple Way in Philadelphia. He heads up Red Letter Christians, a movement of people committed to living 'as if Jesus meant the things he said'. Shane is a champion for grace which has led him into jails advocating for the homeless, and to places like Iraq and Afghanistan to stand against war. Now grace fuels his passion to end the death penalty and eradicate gun violence.

"People tell me all the time, 'my life was such a mess and then I met Jesus,' may God bless them … For me, I pretty much had my life together and then I met Jesus. And I've been recovering ever since." Shane being wonderfully Shane-like on how Jesus turned his life upside down.

Knowing Jesus meant that he knew he was called to action, to prayer and to service; not to add to the "clutter, noise and Christian stuff" (as he describes it), which too often distracts us from the Gospel and Jesus' words. What Shane tries to do day after day is concentrate on what Jesus said: to pray, to be filled with his strength and to do all that he can to see earth be as it is in heaven – beginning with his hometown of North Philadelphia.

Archbishop Justin is a Shane fan. He has admired his work and ministry for over a decade and – although Shane is about the busiest man there is – he and Archbishop Justin are sometimes able to meet: encounters which always leave Archbishop Justin bursting with energy, renewed by Shane's infectious spirit and inspired by all his ideas of how to reimagine the Church.

The Community of St Anselm: Ignacio Fantaguzzi and Joanna Muirhead

Both Ignacio and Joanna are part of the Community of St Anselm; because this is how they both came to know Archbishop Justin, and because we would like to talk a little of the Community, we have placed them together.

✦

Ignacio is an Argentine who has worked in various energy-related companies as an engineer and as a consultant. In 2014 he moved to London and in 2015 he joined the newly formed Community of St Anselm, where he is now a member of the board of trustees. Since April 2018 his work has moved him and his family to Houston, but he is still as active as ever in the community.

✦

Joanna is a partner in a London law firm and was a non-residential member of the Community of St Anselm in 2015/16. Since then she has been continuing her journey by training as a spiritual companion with the Chemin Neuf Community, an ecumenical Roman Catholic community rooted in Ignatian spirituality.

✦

Ignacio Fantaguzzi and Joanna Muirhead both opted to disembark from the all-too-familiar treadmill of work and city life in order to embrace a year of contemplation. They joined (as nonresidential members) the Community of St Anselm, at Lambeth Palace.

As Abbot of the Community, Archbishop Justin hoped this would be a formative chapter in Ignacio and Joanna's lives;

an experience that would impact – and perhaps define – their future decisions and actions. As we read in both their messages, this experience has indeed been woven into their everyday lives, and continues to strengthen their faith. They will forever be part of this growing Community.

The Community began after the newly enthroned Archbishop of Canterbury posed a question to his friends, Sam and Jo Wells: 'How do we turn Lambeth Palace into a place that is known to serve, not to rule?' The answer? 'Start a community.'

And so the Community of St Anselm (CoSA) was founded.

A group of Christians aged 20–35, from every denomination (eliciting quite the reaction in some quarters), was invited to live at Lambeth Palace alongside Archbishop Justin.

The vision for the Community was typical of the Anglican Communion: transform the world, all together, through the love of Jesus Christ.

Some from CoSA are in full-time work, joining the Community for evenings of study and for retreats. Most live here full-time (sleeping in shared rooms), with their days regulated by the ancient monastic rhythm of prayer. Lectures, studying, community projects, retreats (silent or otherwise), spiritual direction and more, are the foundations of a year that will undoubtedly shape them forever. A routine that affords them wonderful opportunities, rich in experience, but is by no means a leisurely year off.

The Religious Life in the Church has, of course, existed for thousands of years. Modelling this tradition, CoSA was never expected to be an easy life: the coexistence of different cultures, denominations and nationalities under one roof (albeit a rather large one), all arriving with wildly differing convictions (both personal and spiritual), brings its challenges. Who cooks what? Who cleans when? How should you receive

Holy Communion? What is the future of the Church? Trivial
or existential, these questions are not avoided in Community
life. Nevertheless, for a year, Community members commit
themselves to one another – to live as a whole. A leap of faith
which brings great rewards.

Dany Cotton

Dany is the first woman to be Commissioner of the London
Fire Brigade. She has served London for more than thirty
years, at every rank, attending major incidents from the
Clapham Rail Crash to the Grenfell Tower Fire.

✦

Leading the London Fire Brigade has never been an easy task.
Our firefighters are permanently on standby across the country
– the only ones among us taught to run into fire, as well as
rescuing people from traffic accidents and other incidents.

For Dany, appointment as Commissioner in September
2016 has thrown up one harrowing challenge after another:
a list of emergencies including the attacks on London Bridge,
Borough Market, Westminster Bridge and Finsbury Park, and
of course, the fire at Grenfell Tower.

The courage and bravery demonstrated by Dany and her
team, facing the full horror of that blaze, was extraordinary.
Archbishop Justin met and spoke with a handful of firefighters
that day and heard just a little of what they had witnessed and
tried desperately to deal with.

When Dany and Archbishop Justin have met at Lambeth
Palace, she has spoken of what her staff do every day serving
London; the Archbishop is always struck by her dedication to
protecting others, and by how proud she is of her team.

Pippa Cramer

An occupational therapist, Pippa has worked for many years in the National Health Service, specialising in neuro-rehabilitation and care of the elderly. In 2011 she founded Connections at Holy Trinity Church, Claygate. She is passionate about sharing God's love with older friends and encouraging other churches in their seniors' ministry.

✦

Pippa is an angel. Archbishop Justin and everyone at Connections say so.

Having heard of Pippa's work, Archbishop Justin asked to join their gathering in 2015, and was met by a buzzing indoor market square of everything you could hope for in order to feel better about the world. There were welcomers offering tea and cake; there were tables where one could collect food parcels to fill a freezer, find help to mend broken hearing aids, understand iPhones and the mysteries of Skype, or print photos of grandchildren. There were places to play board games or cuddle companion dogs, and people to explain local services.

At every table, someone was there to hear how things were going. It is place to revive those who have withdrawn from the world.

Spring 2016 saw a Connections meeting at Lambeth Palace, to which the whole Connections gaggle came en masse – including Bella (the spaniel) and all their usual tables. Archbishop Justin hopes so much that one day we will all know of Connections and, more importantly, where our nearest branch is.

Bishop Michael Curry

Michael B. Curry is the 27th Presiding Bishop of the Episcopal Church; the first African American to hold that post. Previously, he was Bishop of North Carolina for more than fifteen years, after serving parishes in Winston-Salem, Cincinnati and Baltimore. A graduate of Hobart & William Smith Colleges and Yale Divinity School, Bishop Curry is author of *Crazy Christians*, *Songs My Grandma Sang*, and *The Power of Love*.

✦

"Love is the only way . . . Don't underestimate it, don't even oversentimentalise it. There is power, power in love" 19th May 2018, when the world fell in love with Bishop Michael Curry.

He came to Windsor to marry a young couple and – with a voice between speech and song – to bang the drum for the revolution of Jesus.

As Jeremy Vine put it, "the preacher is doing 50 in a 30 zone and it's brilliant."

As one commentator said, our Royal Family had "looks [which] suggest perhaps they aren't familiar with his style of preaching". The BBC, that reliable supply of British understatement, was probably right: this whirlwind of love-radiating preaching is not quite what our monarch and her family (nor the rest of the country) are used to . . . they usually have Archbishop Justin. But the Archbishop himself expected nothing less from his great friend and colleague.

Bishop Michael spoke to us all with the teachings of Martin Luther King; of the power of goodness and of love. He reminded us that we must never for one moment slip into an apathy which underestimates or sentimentalises these greatest of powers.

Because as we read the words in this book – of Bryan, Emmily, Daoud, the Charis team, Robi or Mr Hinton, to name a few – we see the only source of energy that can heal, reconcile and delight: love.

As the Bishop quoted: "Where true love is found, God himself is there."

Robi Damelin

Robi Damelin joined the Parents Circle – Families Forum, a group of bereaved Palestinian and Israeli families working for reconciliation, after her son was killed by a Palestinian sniper.

✦

Robi is part of the Parents Circle – Families Forum, a community founded to connect those who have lost someone to the Israeli–Palestinian conflict – a community which sadly continues to grow. Visit their website and you find these words: 'We are the only association in the world that does not wish to welcome any new members.'

Robi and her Palestinian and Israeli colleagues know the devastation of loss, and their response is remarkable. Through their demonstration of unity and the power of story, they promote peaceful dialogue between sides – a high ambition, considering so many feel any sort of dialogue isn't possible.

Archbishop Justin knows too well the agony of losing a child. To see a collection of people living with such grace, in the face of so much, is overwhelming. He and his wife Caroline went on their second visit to the Holy Land in 2017, where the Parents Circle welcomed Caroline and shared their stories with her at length.

The Revd Jo Davies

Jo is wife to Karl, mother to two adult sons, former curate at Holy Trinity Brompton (HTB) and now Anglican chaplain at HMP Pentonville. She volunteered and then worked for many years with HTB's Ministry of Caring for Ex-Offenders, an organisation group that links men and women coming out of prison with churches and Christian mentors, to support their release into the community.

✦

"That's why I do it. Because I know I couldn't serve a sentence in here. I could not do it." Jo explaining why she has spent her life working in prisons.

Archbishop Justin first visited Pentonville in 2015, spending time with inmates, the prison governor and Imam Suhel (head of the chaplaincy team). Archbishop Justin was also invited to speak at Jo's weekly Alpha session; a discussion group centred around the Bible to which all are welcome (assuming they have the necessary trust of the prison).

Once finished, we all queued to leave the chapel in an orderly and recordable fashion: Lambeth Palace and Chaplaincy teams back to the office, prisoners to their quarters . . . prisoners and the Archbishop. Archbishop Justin had joined the lines returning to the wings. He wanted to see where they lived. We were shown around a few of the unoccupied cells, some of which were for new arrivals: once processed they are watched very closely on their first nights, when the risk of suicide is particularly high. It is of course not an easy place in which to work, yet this is where Jo spends most of her time.

Read about Billy in her message and you'll see how her support surpasses a prison term. For seventeen years she welcomed

him into her life, church, family and home. There was nothing
naive about Jo's affection for Billy – it was a joyful dedication to
welcoming people, no matter what the rest of us think.

Mme Rebecca N. De Mabior

Mme Rebecca Nyandeng de Mabior is the widow of South
Sudan's late revolutionary leader, Dr John Garang de
Mabior. Since her husband died in a helicopter crash in July
2005, Mme Rebecca has been a vocal proponent for peace,
prosperity and development for the people of South Sudan.
For this and other reasons she has been affectionately
dubbed 'the Mother of the Nation'.

✦

Madame Rebecca's message laments her beloved South Sudan.

Her biggest hope for Christmas is to see the country free of
bullets, but the independence its people gained in 2011 gave
only a fleeting spell of hope amid the violence they have been
suffering for so long. Still, Madame Rebecca will never forget
her countrymen – those lost to the war or those forced to flee.
In fact, she is perhaps their greatest champion who, through
her own steadfast grace and calm, is doing all she can to guide
her country away from bloodshed.

After their first meeting, Archbishop Justin describes
feeling mesmerised by her extraordinary absence of bitterness
or anger, and her compelling tenacity to strive for peace.
He considers himself very fortunate to have spent time with
Madame Rebecca on his numerous visits to her country.

This Mother of South Sudan is one of our greatest teachers
of grace.

The Rt. Hon. Tobias Ellwood

Tobias was elected as Member of Parliament for Bournemouth East in May 2005, and subsequently re-elected in 2010, 2015 and most recently in June 2017. He was Parliamentary Under-Secretary of State at the Foreign and Commonwealth Office with special responsibility for the Middle East and Africa from July 2014, and was made Parliamentary Under-Secretary of State in the Ministry of Defence in June 2017.

✦

There is much talk of terrorism these days. Mercifully, the majority of us have not lost someone we love to it, but Tobias has. His brother Jon, a teacher, was killed when a bomb ripped through a Bali nightclub in 2002.

In May this year, Tobias was invited to speak at the National Memorial Arboretum in Staffordshire. The Ellwood family were among the three hundred guests, all of whom had lost people to terrorism abroad. They were there to dedicate a memorial entitled Still Water, *created to offer a place of peace in which to reflect. Archbishop Justin was asked to lead the ceremony and, like everyone else present, was struck by Tobias' words and how determined he was to stand up to violence and hatred – a determination only strengthened by the attack on Westminster in March 2017. This was an attack that Tobias not only witnessed, but in which he tried to save of one of its victims, PC Keith Palmer.*

Whether at home or abroad, Tobias is more aware than most of the impact of terrorism; something which underlines his work in Parliament.

Julie Etchingham

Julie Etchingham is anchor of ITV's *News at Ten* and *Tonight* programmes. In her career as a journalist, she has worked for BBC News, Sky News and ITN. She is married with two sons.

✦

Julie is a regular visitor to Lambeth Palace.

In the autumn of 2016, she accompanied Archbishop Justin on his official visit to Pope Francis in Rome. Spending time together, two things struck Archbishop Justin about this very able journalist: Julie's evident knowledge of, and devotion to, her Roman Catholic Church; and that he was never going to get off lightly in her interviews … Except perhaps in May this year, when Julie interviewed him and Bishop Michael Curry before the Royal Wedding. That time, watching the three of them sitting in the grounds at Windsor in the sunshine, it was difficult to tell who was having the most fun.

Father Laurent Fabre

After receiving the baptism of the Holy Spirit in 1973, Father Laurent founded the Chemin Neuf Community, which now has a presence in thirty-two countries. Ever since, he has had a passion for the unity of the Church. He is regularly invited to teach in various international gatherings, where he testifies to the work of the Holy Spirit in the world.

✦

People of faith are no more immune to divisions than anyone else. Between the millions of Christians worldwide, there are many denominations, with all the likely complexities you'd expect from a vast number of human beings trying to get along.

Without people like Father Laurent, such division would far too often overcome the good and obscure the joy and glory of each group. A Jesuit priest, Father Laurent has given his life to the unity of the Church, and in 1973 he founded the Chemin Neuf Community. This Roman Catholic Community had an ecumenical vocation from the start: Lutherans, Anglicans, Roman Catholics, Pentecostals and more – all granted equal status and rights – were to live together; to serve the Church together.

Archbishop Justin met Father Laurent about fifteen years ago and was so impacted by his ministry that, on becoming Archbishop of Canterbury, he invited members of the Chemin Neuf Community to live at Lambeth Palace – to be its bedrock of prayer.

As Archbishop Justin says, "there has never, in history, been a renewal of the Church without a renewal of the religious life."

Sarah Giles

Sarah began working as Jonathan Bryan's home education teacher four years ago. She has been privileged to witness his 'unlocking' and honoured to be asked to become a trustee of his charity, Teach Us Too, which works to improve literacy education for children like him and promote the teaching of literacy to all, regardless of their labels.

✦

When Archbishop Justin and Jonathan Bryan first met a few years ago, at an event in the Bristol Diocese, they couldn't have a conversation. Jonathan's physical immobility meant he'd been taught only the basics of reading; he could recognise a few letters and his name. When they were reunited this year, however, Archbishop Justin and Jonathan were able to talk about all sorts of things – something that Sarah helped make possible, with an alphabet board and years of faithful dedication.

It is impossible to quantify what Sarah's teaching has helped unlock. Now a published author, Jonathan is testament to the potential being wasted in so many children and adults who are still yet to join the conversation; who haven't had the same opportunity to be released. The charity that she has cofounded, Teach Us Too, is addressing just that; injecting an essential surge of urgency to the cause – that everyone must have the same educational opportunities.

Grace
Member of the Charis Tiwala community.

✦

Grace and Archbishop Justin first shared a pot of tea in 2015, on his initial visit to Charis Tiwala. Before we arrived, the group thought that either the Pope or, in Laila's case, Justin Bieber, was coming for tea. They managed their disappointment well. In fact, so wonderful was our time together that since this first tea, Grace, Laila, Katie and all at Charis have become a cherished part of the community at Lambeth Palace.

They come, not often enough, for Bible studies and supper with Archbishop Justin; for cups of tea in the garden (Laila is a big fan of the rope swing on the tree); and to every Christmas carol service – a tradition that would be incomplete without them all.

Rupert Grey

Rupert has balanced life in the law courts with long periods in the wild places of the earth. As a lawyer he has represented national papers, politicians, celebrities, photographers, publishers, bankers and explorers. As an outdoorsman and photographer he has travelled on foot, by boat, dog sled, camel, elephant and vintage Rolls Royce in many different parts of the world, including Papua New Guinea, Alaska and the South Pacific. He is frequently accompanied by his wife Jan and three daughters. Rupert serves on the board of a number of frontline charities in the fields of performing arts, education, photography and conservation. His photographs have been exhibited in several countries, including Bangladesh, and his articles have been widely published.

Between his legal and charity work and human rights campaigns, Rupert is a chronicler, photographer and traveller. If he's not tending his fields and barns at home, he's likely to be found preparing his 1930s Rolls Royce for its next great adventure – the last of which took him and his beloved wife, Jan, from Mumbai to Bangladesh. This glorious combination of passions has seen him providing legal advice from some unusual settings. His most recent email read: 'Am on a most beautiful timber boat moored in a remote and empty harbour in the north Pacific. It's absolutely freezing'; whilst he apologised in another telephone call: "Hold on. Sheep escaped. And [presumably unrelated] British High Commission calling."

Despite all this, Rupert has found time to give us his invaluable advice (including calming encouragement when faced with the unknown world of publishing). Without him, this book would not exist.

He is a lawyer of some forty years – devoted to freedom of speech, human rights, the right to privacy, intellectual property rights and justice. One of his most important battles has been the worldwide effort to liberate Dr Shahidul Alam – a grave injustice against a man of the highest integrity; a worry and loss felt most deeply by Rupert as Shahidul is his dear friend.

This sense of loss is acute, but not unusual. The refusal to accept injustices is something he shares with Archbishop Justin. Indeed, Rupert's first visit to Lambeth Palace was to hear another mightily impressive lawyer, Bryan Stevenson, lecture and be interviewed by the Archbishop – a combination that afforded the Archbishop quite the duo of legal minds.

Bear Grylls

One of the most recognised faces worldwide in survival and outdoor adventure, Bear Grylls began his journey in 21 SAS (Special Air Service) before becoming one of the youngest ever climbers of Mount Everest. The TV host, honoured by BAFTA, is also a number-one bestselling author, Chief Scout to sixty million worldwide, and an Honorary Colonel in the Royal Marine Commandos.

✦

We know a lot about Bear. He was in the SAS, strands himself on islands, eats the odd carcass as he travels, crosses gorges on zip wires and challenges movie stars and presidents to do the same. He is also Chief Scout.

Bear and the Scouts seem a natural fit – roaming the great outdoors and building fires. Well, yes … but there is so much more to it than that. As Chief Scout, Bear leads sixty million girls and boys across two hundred countries – young people of

*all races, all faiths and none, and every conceivable culture
and demographic. Even in the toughest and most vulnerable
parts of our world there are, as Bear says, Scouts being taught
to serve: from Aleppo, where they help the UN distribute aid, to
London, building community gardens, and to rural Pakistan,
where Scouts are trained to offer first aid in otherwise isolated
regions. In each place, the Scouts offer a sense of adventure,
community and belonging. It is no wonder that there are
thousands on a waiting list to join in the UK alone.*

*Archbishop Justin is always struck by his seemingly limitless
energy, how generous he is with his time, and his devotion to
ensuring that future generations are encouraged and valued.*

*As Bear reminded our Government last year, "the engine
house [of our country] doesn't lie in the corridors of Westminster.
It just doesn't. The engine house is with young people."*

Miranda Hart

Miranda Hart is an award-winning writer and actress. Beyond
the comedy she became well known for, her writing includes
articles, memoirs, the children's novel *The Girl with the Lost
Smile*, and *Miranda's Daily Dose of Such Fun* in aid of her
Comic Relief Fund, which supports and guides people with
anxiety and depression towards emotional well-being.

✦

*The Girl with the Lost Smile introduces us to Chloe, a girl
who is trying to find her smile again. Chloe is one of Miranda's
most recent creations and is a story to share with children in
that often-baffling process of trying to become happy again, to
smile again. The veneration of gentleness Miranda writes about
is obvious when you read this offering to children.*

Her stardom was found through her hilarious, pony skipping, 'such fun' sitcom Miranda, so it can be easy to assume that life for her — for comedic actors in general — is a riot of nonstop laughter. But of course, that isn't always the case. It was discussing vulnerability such as anxiety and other life experiences, after a brief introduction a few years ago, that kept her in touch with Archbishop Justin; sharing how we might, gently, better support ourselves and those around us.

Miranda's empathy is a wonderful gift to offer others. Yes, Miranda can make 15,000 people laugh at the O2 Arena, but she has always made sure her work is underpinned by messages and ways to connect our universal vulnerabilities. Chloe is one way that she speaks to our younger friends.

Anthony Ray Hinton

Anthony Ray Hinton, a community educator at the Equal Justice Initiative, was falsely accused of committing two murders outside of Birmingham, Alabama, in 1985. He was wrongly convicted and spent nearly thirty years on Alabama's death row before he was exonerated and freed in April 2015. A deeply compelling speaker, he has become a powerful advocate against the death penalty and speaks across the United States about the urgent need for criminal justice reform.

✦

Like so many of Bryan Stevenson's clients, Anthony Ray Hinton should never have needed a lawyer. For thirty years he was kept in a 5 x 7 foot cell, threatened with execution for twenty-eight years.

He hadn't committed a crime. Terribly, to the prosecutor

that was not important. For reasons we will never truly know or comprehend, all that was important was that somebody went to prison. For a young black man in Alabama in 1985, the odds were stacked against Mr Hinton.

In his book, The Sun Does Shine, *he shares the horror of his experiences and provides a glimpse of the tiny cell in which he lived. Although he talks of the pain and misery he and his family suffered, there is no hint of malice or vengefulness. Mr Hinton was robbed of half a lifetime, yet still chronicles the love and warmth he found in his friends and the moments of joy and peace he somehow managed to create on death row.*

Archbishop Justin first heard of Mr Hinton's case when he met Bryan in 2015. Despite Mr Hinton never meeting Archbishop Justin in person, he has been generous enough to contribute to this book. We have our fingers crossed that one day he will be able to come to Lambeth Palace.

Afua Hirsch
Afua Hirsch writes, speaks and broadcasts on themes of identity, belonging, justice and social and cultural change. She is a columnist for The Guardian, and regular broadcaster on the BBC, Sky News, CNN, and Channel 4. Her bestselling first book *Brit(ish)* was published in 2018 by Jonathan Cape and won the Royal Society of Literature Jerwood Prize.

✦

Afua's mother's family are from Ghana, having on one side originally fled from the Ashanti Kingdom during the British colonial war. Afua's father is British and Jewish; his family fled Eastern Europe to escape the Nazis. Afua is a mixed-race

British woman with Ghanian, Jewish and British history. For her, the simple, simple question, 'where are you from?' has a complicated response; but working it out led her to write the best-selling book, Brit(ish).

So often we curl up at the mention of 'race' or 'identity'. Many try to avoid tricky subjects and controversy; but not Afua. To the dismay of the Church's Press Office, nor does Archbishop Justin. This made for a very enjoyable first meeting. She and Archbishop Justin don't agree on all things, of course, but never has that stopped a good conversation. It is in the talking, the debating, the writing and shaping of our thoughts that progress can come. Afua's is one of those voices that won't let us rest on our laurels.

Dorothy Horn

Following the death of her husband in March 2015, Dorothy's family encouraged her to start attending Connections at Holy Trinity Church, Claygate. In the three years since then, great-grandmother Dorothy has been on a journey which has enabled her to form new and special friendships and significantly deepened her relationship with God.

When Archbishop Justin met Dorothy at Connections he was struck hugely by the warmth and devotion with which she supports others. A few weeks after this, Dorothy spoke at the Lambeth Palace carol service. She explained how hard it had been to lose her Tom after sixty-three years of marriage and how terribly lonely she had become after he died – quite something to share so frankly with an archbishop and a room full of strangers.

Her brave words were an amazing testament to what

happens when someone like Pippa welcomes you into a community; someone who calls in the evenings to check in, or includes you in gatherings of friends.

There is so much wasted potential among the elderly community, who are often overlooked simply because of their age. Dorothy, at 89, is now a regular volunteer; supporting many who are twenty years her junior, so that they too can find a new home – as she did.

Ellis Jones

✦

Autumn 2014, and Youthscape celebrated the opening of their new building. Well, the 'nearly opening' … Archbishop Justin dodged the odd hanging cable and hopped between scaffolding boards over holes in the ground when being shown around.

It was as clear then, as it is now, that what Youthscape had built was a home for the young people they support – not built to be a fancy centre, but a building with a large kitchen and living room at its heart: places to eat and be together.

Invited to join their service and party, Archbishop Justin spoke at the event – an evening cohosted brilliantly by the then 17-year-old Ellis. A few weeks after this, Ellis spoke at the carol service at Lambeth Palace about the different Christmases she had had, some alone, and what Youthscape had given her: family.

Over the years, Ellis (now a member of the Community of St Anselm) and others from Youthscape have been back to eat and talk with Archbishop Justin, where he has faced rapid-fire questioning about his work and the Bible, and been reproached by Ellis for not introducing her to Prince Harry in time.

John F. Kerry

John F. Kerry served as the United States' sixty-eighth Secretary of State from 2013 to 2017. A US Senator for Massachusetts from 1985 to 2013, he chaired the Senate Foreign Relations Committee from 2009 to 2013. He served in the US Navy, completing two tours of duty in Vietnam, receiving a Silver Star, a Bronze Star with Combat V, and three Purple Hearts. He is the bestselling author of *A Call to Service: My Vision for a Better America*, *This Moment on Earth*, and a memoir, *Every Day Is Extra*. He is the Distinguished Fellow for Global Affairs at Yale University; and the Visiting Distinguished Statesman for the Carnegie Endowment for International Peace.

✦

Archbishop Justin has become friends with Secretary Kerry … without us really noticing.

This may be because he knows we would be terribly curious (nosey) and deeply envious. Or because despite our best efforts, he sometimes slips from our radar to enjoy time with others outside of his tightly scheduled and meticulously briefed life.

Following Secretary Kerry's work, it is not difficult to imagine why they chose to cross paths. There are subjects that create what we refer to here as a 'Justin-shaped hole' – a space of world affairs, God, the economy, the Middle East, western Africa, bridging divides … conversations to which we lose our Archbishop, knowing it will be a while until he resurfaces or is nudged to go to his next meeting. How many discussions there must be for the two of them to disappear into.

Secretary Kerry is known to the rest of us as one of his country's most distinguished veterans, politicians and diplomats; a political giant whose voice no longer speaks from the

Administration but still seeks to inform and guide us. A survivor of the war in Vietnam, he has worked – since the moment his feet were back on safe soil – to keep the world at peace; he warns us that puffed-up rhetoric can lead nowhere sensible and nowhere (literally) safe. He persistently reminds us that the horrors of war are real and lasting and to be avoided at all costs.

But this voice of reason is no partisan. Read his tribute to a fellow giant, the late Senator John McCain, and you will read a beautiful farewell to a friend – a message that reverberates with profound respect for someone with whom he held so many deep differences.

Respect amidst difference; something which Archbishop Justin admires in John Kerry and in many others – the shared endeavour to express our diversity always, with kindness and with grace.

The Rt. Hon. Sadiq Khan

Sadiq Khan was elected Mayor of London in May 2016. Before this, Sadiq had a distinguished career as the Member of Parliament for Tooting, a constituency in south London. He served as a Minister in both the Department for Communities and Local Government and the Department for Transport under Prime Minister Gordon Brown. Later he served as the Shadow Secretary of State for Justice and the Shadow Minister for London.

✦

"This is London! Breaking my fast with the Chief Rabbi and Archbishop Justin & young Londoners of many faiths #Ramadan." Sadiq's tweet as he celebrated an Iftar at Lambeth Palace, eating together with the Archbishop of Canterbury,

Chief Rabbi Emphraim Mirvis and a wonderful group of young people.

The photo included in this tweet was a selfie, showing Lambeth's Great Hall packed with smiling faces. It flew around the Twittersphere and was retweeted by J.K. Rowling with the words: "This picture gives me hope. Actually, I've got something quite large in my eye ..."

Rowling was not alone in welcoming this reminder – that friends, colleagues and leaders of different faiths do eat and work (and laugh) together. A reality shared in synagogues, churches, mosques, temples, meeting houses and faith centres every day, all over the world.

Emmily Koiti

Human and civil rights activist. Youth representative in South Sudan's peace process.

✦

Emmily is a young South Sudanese woman; a doctor, active member of her local church and an activist with a pivotal role in the South Sudan Young Leaders Forum – a group integral to the country's international peace.

Virginia Gamba, UN Special Representative, believes South Sudan is "a country where youth must help to bring back values – remember what being a human is all about". This is no platitude. In a place where war, violence and chaos have reigned for so long, returning to humanity, restoring dignity and living in peace are tasks to which people like Emmily have dedicated themselves, despite the great risks involved.

Archbishop Justin is always deeply moved to hear of those like Emmily who are devoted to reconciliation, patiently giving *kindness the chance to overcome hate. He travels to South Sudan to speak with those affected and offers what he can: friendship, witness and counsel. For the country's leaders, he helps forge connections to other faith leaders across the world, through the eighty-million-strong network of the Anglican Communion.*

At Lambeth Palace this Christmas, as always, prayers will be said for South Sudan: prayers for peace; for strength to be given to those trying to create it.

Sally Lloyd-Jones

Sally Lloyd-Jones is a New York Times bestselling writer and sometimes a performer of her work. Born in, and raised across, Africa and in a boarding school in the New Forest (basically Hogwarts before Hogwarts), she studied at the Sorbonne, worked in London and now lives in New York City.

✦

Children's Bibles are too often charmless, laughless texts – the Bible stripped bare of challenge and wonder. Not so with The Jesus Story Book Bible; *Sally's book is something to be treasured. Her extraordinary ability to communicate with children infuses the Gospel with wonder and humour: Jonah in a grump because he didn't want the job God had for him; James, Matthew and Peter squabbling over who was the nicest and cleverest and so would be most loved, only to be shown – by little children – that those things don't matter because we are all loved the same. Jesus, having brought Jairus's daughter back from the dead, knew exactly what the little girl needed next – breakfast and a hug. It is not just small people who become enchanted by these stories; grown-ups are often to be found curled up with this book as well.*

Archbishop Justin and Sally first knew one another many moons ago in Paris but are now back in touch working together on a new project … Watch this space.

Jo Malone CBE

After discovering a talent for creating scented products by hand in her kitchen, in 1994 Jo launched her first brand, Jo Malone London. In 1999, Jo sold her business to Estée Lauder and remained Creative Director until 2006. In 2011, she launched a new brand, Jo Loves. She was made a Commander of the Order of the British Empire (CBE) in the 2018 Queen's Birthday Honours List for her services to the British Economy and the GREAT Britain campaign, which promotes British creativity and industry on the international stage. She contributes to consumer publications and appears regularly on radio and TV.

✦

The Jo Malone brand is on high streets all over the world. Not bad for a girl who grew up on a council estate in Bexleyheath, without so many of the privileges which help launch careers. At school, dyslexic and unable to keep up in the 'normal' way, Jo was labelled lazy and stupid. Of course, she was neither. Fast-forward twenty years and Jo sold her global empire in 1999. A condition of sale was to leave the cosmetics market for a few years – a tough wait for a self-proclaimed control freak, who describes driving everyone mad, from her husband to directors of the boards on which she sat. But then she was back, building her next business Jo Loves.

Jo and Archbishop Justin – both financial pages fanatics – have much to discuss when they meet, including the age-old conundrum of serving both God and mammon. Archbishop Justin finds her tenacity and no-nonsense approach hugely refreshing, especially when it is applied to encouraging others.

Jarrod McKenna

Jarrod McKenna is the founder of the Common Grace and First Home Project for refugees. One of the instigators of the #LoveMakesAWay movement, Jarrod is also the cohost of two popular Australian podcasts on contemplative prayer and liberation, the *InVerse Podcast* and the *Perisson Podcast*.

✦

Jarrod is a priest, writer, activist and a general pain to those trying to maintain the status quo. Achievements which were not necessarily (apart from the latter) on the cards when he was at school: dyslexia, ADHD and frustration meant life was sometimes challenging. Through this, his parents were patient and faithful; part of a home church, they baptised him in the family pool. So his faith was rooted at home, a privilege of which he knows the value.

As Jarrod is based in Australia, his visits to Lambeth Palace are somewhat limited. Archbishop Justin follows his work from afar and admires not only his tenacious spirit but the measured and polite way in which he speaks.

And speak he must. Children locked in indefinite detention is not something Jarrod finds acceptable. But rather than not finding it acceptable and then getting on with life anyway, he is doing what he can to bring about change. He acknowledges that we face difficult and complex issues, but believes that we must not hide from these issues. Because if a child is locked in cell, we haven't yet got it right.

The Very Revd Canon Hosam Naoum

Dean Hosam is the first indigenous Dean of Jerusalem. He was installed on Ascension Day, 2012. In addition to his ministry at St George's Cathedral, Jerusalem, Dean Hosam serves as the Secretary of the Patriarchs and Heads of Churches in Jerusalem. In 2016, Dean Hosam was appointed and installed as an Honorary Canon at Rochester Cathedral, UK. Dean Hosam is finishing his Doctoral Degree at the Virginia Theological Seminary, USA.

✦

Hosam began his Church life as a vicar in the West Bank, ministering to three parish churches. His theological studies have taken him around the world but, despite numerous job offers in 'easier' settings, his pursuit of learning always brings him back home. He doesn't want to learn more in order to leave his homeland; he wants to learn more to increase the impact he can have by staying.

As Dean of St George's Cathedral, Hosam works with his Archbishop, Suheil Dawani, and other priests from across the diocese. He is often found in Gaza: checking in with the hospitals that the cathedral supports, greeting the latest patients and offering counsel, Holy Communion and chatter.

It was this devotion – this dedication to being a priest amid the conflict – that Archbishop Justin so admired when they first met in 2007, through the Community of the Cross of Nails. They quickly made friends and have often worked together since, in particular during the Archbishop's visits to the Holy Land.

Hosam lived for some time at a seminary in South Africa, where he came to know Archbishop Desmond Tutu; who, when he heard of Hosam's home and family, would greet him, using the now precious nickname, "Ah, the son of a carpenter from Nazareth."

Daoud Nassar

Daoud is the Director of *Tent of Nations*, an educational and environmental family farm in Bethlehem.

✦

In the hills of the Holy Land, the Tent of Nations farm might seem an idyllic place of rural life, but this is the West Bank where little is straightforward and daily life is fraught with the consequences of conflict.

Daoud, however, is clear that he will not hate, and he will not fight. Instead, he and his family choose to devote themselves to the land and encourage their thousands of visitors to do the same. Welcoming Jews, agnostics, Muslims, athiests and Christians, Daoud uses his farm as a way to reconnect people with the land – to help, as he says, "lay the foundations for peace". Tending to his olive trees and goats, living a life as normal as his situation allows, Daoud is an example of extraordinary hope in a region so saddened by conflict.

On his visit to the Holy Land, Archbishop Justin was welcomed by Daoud. He was profoundly moved by the capacity of this remarkable man, and his community, to show gentle love whatever the daily pressures and hardships. It is people like Daoud from whom Archbishop Justin draws inspiration and renewed strength, to face hardship with grace.

David Nott

A London consultant surgeon, David has worked since 1993 as a volunteer surgeon in many of the world's most challenging and dangerous natural disaster and war zones. In 2015 he set up the David Nott Foundation with his wife, Elly, to train doctors in life-saving surgical skills.

✦

In David's message we read of his search for Maram, a five-month-old Syrian baby horribly injured when her home was under siege in Aleppo.

She survived, thanks to David's operation. He then tried desperately to discover how and where she was – routine post-operative care if you aren't in a war zone; a desperate challenge if you are. This says so much about what makes David remarkable. He has offered his help as a surgeon in some of the most dangerous places in our world, training doctors in overstretched hospitals and helping them deal with traumatic injuries.

David repeatedly speaks out, trying to call to account the powerful in Syria, urging them not to turn a blind eye to the suffering of the innocent. During the Christmas of 2017, he helped orchestrate the audacious attempt to secure the safe passage of wounded and sick children from Aleppo's hospitals, having to negotiate with the Assad regime.

Archbishop Justin met David and his wife Elly last year at an event in Lambeth Palace; he was overwhelmed to hear of the work they both do with their foundation – how they will not abandon areas of the world which seem most forsaken.

Sally Phillips

Award-winning actress and writer Sally is well known for her roles in *Alan Partridge*, *Smack the Pony* and the *Bridget Jones* trilogy. She also fronted a BBC documentary, *A World Without Down's Syndrome?* in which she explored the emotionally charged debate around the new DNA screening test that is said to detect Down's in 98 per cent of pregnancies and asked what effect the test could have on society. *A World Without Down's Syndrome?* has won awards and been screened around the world, sparking debate and similar documentaries in many other countries. Sally has become an advocate for Disability Rights, speaking widely on issues that affect her son's community. She has two other children and prefers comedy to ranting.

✦

"We used to screen for Down's syndrome because life with Down's syndrome was short and hard. Now we screen because life is long and the presumed burden is costly, and that's a profound ethical shift in priorities that's gone largely unnoticed. Nobody knows what to do with that." An extract from Sally's address to the Church of England's General Synod.

Hers was a not a talk on being Christian or the issues of terminations; it was on the discussions around those living with Down's, the tests available to detect it during pregnancy, and the language used when parents are first told their baby has the syndrome. Sally spoke alongside Heidi Crowter, a woman with Down's herself, who hopes that parents will no longer see a baby diagnosed with the syndrome as 'bad news'.

Mother to Olly and a friend to many in the Down's community, Sally has written and spoken of her own hope to see more of us pausing to consider where we stand on these issues.

Archbishop Justin was as moved by her Synod address as everyone else listening, and would encourage others to watch the BBC documentary she filmed on the issue.

Matt Redman

Writer of many worship songs, including the Grammy award-winning *10,000 Reasons*, Matt has travelled with his music all around the world to countries including Japan, South Africa, Brazil, Australia and the Czech Republic. Matt is married to Beth, and they have five children.

✦

Matt is a singer. Archbishop Justin is tone deaf. Wonderfully, this has not put a dampener on their friendship.

Whether to lead worship or sing, Matt is so often the one Archbishop Justin invites to join him; in Canterbury Cathedral, at a Welby wedding, broadcasting with the BBC or in the Crypt Chapel at Lambeth Palace. He loves Matt's words and songs, which have become a part of life for so many millions of people all across the globe over the last thirty years. Even the Archbishop wonders about singing (sort of) Matt's songs to himself.

What Archbishop Justin respects and esteems most is Matt's humility and service to others; and his undivided heart for God.

Lieutenant Pete Reed OBE

Pete joined the Royal Navy in 1999 and found the sport of rowing as part of his initial sea training. His military career went in an unintended but wonderful direction in sport. He was made an Officer of the Order of the British Empire (OBE) in 2017. Pete loves photography, adventure, mentoring athletes and telling his story – which will form the basis of the next chapter after rowing.

✦

At 20 years old, serving in the Royal Navy, Pete had a go at rowing. On taking up a new sport, most would be content to learn the basics and perhaps eventually become proficient. Not Pete. This new sport altered the direction of his life: three

Olympic and five World Championship golds are just some of the medals he has earned.

Pete did once talk us through the average Olympian's training regime; an inconceivable schedule to almost all of us. The dedication, will, strength and team spirit required to sustain such a life really is extraordinary. However, it takes its toll. At 37, with overused and bashed joints, Pete (no doubt to the enormous relief of his competitors) retired. What happens next is the big question.

He and Archbishop Justin met at a Navy dinner a while ago and their conversations have continued in all sorts of directions: the ethics of sport, rowing (to our amazement there is a sport Archbishop Justin knows – he coxed at Cambridge), the Church, charities and life in general.

It is wonderful to have an Olympian join the Lambeth Palace community – not least because he was available, when the lift broke just before our biggest service of the year, to carry extremely heavy things down stairs . . .

Fiona Ruttle

Fiona, who has spent fourteen years on the chaplaincy team in a prison, is cowriting a course, *Holding Difficult Conversations*, and is a trustee of the Community of St Anselm.

✦

No one has a life free of conflict.

It starts so early: siblings squabbling, railing against their parents; teenage turmoil, wounding with everything from words to knives; arguments and accusations that split friendships, churches, marriages, families and more.

Fiona, a trained mediator, puts herself in the middle of

conflicts. She doesn't expect to shut them down neatly, or cast judgements sending everyone back to their own corners; nor does she turn up with a half-baked mantra of 'let's get on'.

Instead, with years of practice sitting neutrally in the turmoil, Fiona seeks to interrupt the lock-in pattern of shout, repeat, ignore. Mediators are not there to shift the energy of conflict around, but to transform it.

Along with her husband Stephen (also a mediator), Fiona has joined Archbishop Justin on his mission to encourage reconciliation through the Church across the world. They both share the conviction that difference is not the problem – that is just being human. The problem is when our deep differences are not understood or respected.

So much unhappiness is rooted in conflict; we so desperately need the wisdom of mediators, need people like Fiona, to teach us how to understand the joy and hope of reconciliation.

Elif Shafak

British-Turkish novelist Elif Shafak is an award-winning author, public speaker and a women's rights and human rights activist.

✦

Elif creates stories that remind us of how to be human.

There is no subject this great wordsmith will not address. Hers is a thoughtful, creative voice that is always – even on the most contentious issues – gentle, perceptive and kind. To sit with one of her novels is to nestle into a patchwork of tales, stitched together with her inherent skill, observation and warmth. She has written in almost every genre, entranced by the beauty of language since childhood, and can seemingly write her way into anything, sweeping us along with her.

Elif often reminds us of the danger when nuance is denied; her determination to preserve it is what makes her commentary so urgently necessary, for as she says, "extremist ideologies need each other: Islamophobia in the West relies on anti-Western sentiments in the East. They need each other. They breed each other."

She and Archbishop Justin were introduced a couple of years ago. Since then, Elif has been back to Lambeth Palace, where she and the Archbishop have discussed many things, including the balance of faith and doubt.

Canon Sarah Snyder

A theologian and trained mediator, Sarah has worked for more than thirty years to promote faith-based reconciliation among senior leaders and emerging generations. She leads efforts by the Anglican Communion, under Archbishop Justin Welby, to transform conflict in dangerous, violent parts of our world. Alongside this, she is the Founding Director of the Rose Castle Foundation, an international reconciliation centre.

✦

Archbishop Justin knew in seconds that Sarah was the one to lead his Reconciliation Ministry. For her interview, in the now familiar way, she had come bounding into his study filled with passion and commitment to restoring relationships. It was clear that she had a gift. Combine this with the great skill she has developed over thirty years, and the Archbishop had quite a tour de force to join his staff.

Sarah's dedication has taken her all over the world: South Sudan, Sri Lanka, Pakistan, America and the Middle East are just some of the regions in which she has worked to create *deeper understanding within and between faiths. Whether in the UN, a tent in Timbuktu, or tucked away in a tiny chapel, Sarah has witnessed the transformation that happens when human beings realise their potential for peace.*

She and Archbishop Justin are on a mission: to live out Jesus' calling to be a reconciler, and to encourage others — especially the younger generation — to see what happens when we put our faith into action. Together they are developing a course for local churches through which they hope to build a worldwide movement of peacemakers and ambassadors of reconciliation.

Ambitious? Absolutely. However, Sarah, with her faith in Jesus' teaching and her infectious delight in working with others, is about the only person the Archbishop knows who could pull off such a feat.

Charlie Spencer

When he retired as Theatre Critic for the Daily Telegraph, Charlie suffered an identity crisis and struggled with severe depression. He initially came to Connections as a 'chair mover' and to help with the weekly set-up. Since then he has grown to find peace and purpose as a valued member of the team, listening to and spending time alongside the elderly guests.

✦

Charlie has quite possibly seen more plays than anyone else in London. Four or five shows a week multiplied by thirty-seven years builds an extraordinary repertoire.

It is difficult to comprehend just how much he knows about theatre — actors, writings, directors and their productions. His understanding of how we express ourselves through the arts is remarkable. Yet this oracle of the theatre retired young – not yet 60 and feeling burnt-out and, as he bravely shared, a bit lost to depression.

Along came Pippa, and now Charlie is an essential part of the team who make Connections possible – something Archbishop Justin saw for himself when he met Charlie in 2015. Charlie's story reminds us what can grow from welcoming someone into a community, even if it's as simple as them arranging the furniture. Because it isn't just moving chairs. It's joining others and offering what we are able to bring, alongside our struggles.

This summer, Connections excelled themselves: they brought the beach to their church, for those unable to make it to the sea – ice creams, deckchairs and sand all taken indoors (minus the seagulls and annoying gusts of wind). Charlie, as always, part of the scene.

Bryan Stevenson

Founder and Executive Director of the Equal Justice Initiative (EJI), Bryan Stevenson is a widely acclaimed public interest lawyer who has dedicated his career to helping the poor, the incarcerated and the condemned. He is the author of the New York Times bestseller, *Just Mercy*. Under his leadership, the EJI has established the Legacy Museum: From Enslavement to Mass Incarceration, and a national memorial to victims of lynching, the National Memorial for Peace and Justice, both in Montgomery, Alabama.

✦

"The opposite of poverty is not wealth; the opposite of poverty is justice." Words Bryan has spoken all over the world in his

mission to serve those who have been rejected and forgotten.

The office of the Equal Justice Initiative, founded by Bryan, is based on Commerce Street, Montgomery; so named as it was once a booming market of trade – where African men, women and children were sold to buyers from across the country. It is here that Bryan devotes his life to fighting racial injustice and the incarceration of far too many Americans; many of them black.

Bryan is encouraging his country to address its history of racial inequality, slavery and lynching. He has built a memorial: six acres of space in which to remember and reflect upon the reign of racial terror which, between 1877 and 1950 alone, claimed the lives of more than 4,400 African Americans.

In 2015, Bryan delivered a lecture at Lambeth Palace and was interviewed by Archbishop Justin, who was simply astonished to hear of his work.

Bryan shared many stories; this was one. On his first visit to death row thirty-odd years ago, as an anxious law student, he was tasked with telling an inmate that for the moment there was no risk of execution. The response? Weighed down by shackles, and wrestled back to his cell by guards, the man threw his head back and began to sing an old hymn:

I'm pressing on the upward way
New heights I'm gaining every day;
Still praying as I onward bound,
Lord, plant my feet on higher ground.

This caused the shift in Bryan's understanding and issued the call to his life's work:

"My journey to higher ground was tied to his journey to higher ground; if he didn't get there I wouldn't get there either."

Alan Titchmarsh MBE

Alan Titchmarsh left school at 15 for a career in horticulture. He has written around fifty books on subjects as varied as gardening, natural history and the monarchy, as well as three volumes of autobiography and eleven novels. He broadcasts frequently on television and radio, hosted an ITV chat show for eight years, and now hosts a Saturday morning Classic FM show. Alan was made a Member of Order of the British Empire (MBE) in the millennium New Year Honours and is a Deputy Lieutenant of Hampshire.

Archbishop Justin can't remember where he met Alan, or when he first came to Lambeth Palace (or in fact anything that was helpful to begin this piece).

But as with all growing friendships, this is no matter. Now a member of one of the Archbishop's Bible study groups, Alan has become a regular visitor to Lambeth Palace. To show Archbishop Justin a schedule carrying Alan's name is to cheer him up because he just really enjoys his company – for his humour, his humanity and his gentle but steady faith.

Alan offers his perspectives generously, but never forcefully, and there is much that Archbishop Justin enjoys discussing with him – from goodness to evangelism, from the Anglican Communion to gardening. The latter came up (somehow) during an evening here, and Alan's host began asking him for gardening advice. Since the conversation was supposed to be on the Prodigal Son, Alan very kindly steered the Archbishop back to the Bible.

Hea Woo

Hea Woo was imprisoned for four years in a North Korean camp for her faith but through this trial she experienced the love of God. Hea's husband was martyred in North Korea for his Christian faith at the hands of the regime.

✦

'Do not try to escape. You will be killed'. The sign on the gates of the North Korean labour camp where Hea Woo was held.

Her story is laced with unimaginable horrors. After she lost her daughter to starvation and her husband was killed by the Secret Police for escaping to China, Hea Woo herself sought to flee. However, she too was caught and sent to a labour camp. Hea Woo lived out her punishment toiling in the fields, surviving on only a few spoons of rice a day in what she describes as "a living hell".

When Archbishop Justin heard of Hea Woo's experiences, he was stunned. He has been able to worship and celebrate his faith all over the world. Hea Woo had put herself in extraordinary danger to do the same; in the airless toilets of that awful place. Who knows, perhaps this Christmas a similar group will be in the same place, meeting to celebrate their faith in God.

Sharing Hea Woo's story is not intended to dampen or sadden your Christmas – quite the opposite. It is precisely the hope and joy that Hea Woo describes which we are celebrating – a love so powerful that, even for a minute, it can bring light to a place of such darkness.

To be read on Christmas Eve ...

A Note before Christmas

My dear friends,

'For God so loved the world that he gave his only Son, so that everyone who believes in him may not perish but may have eternal life.' (John 3: 16 NRSV)

Friends, at its core, Christmas is the way of love.

Jesus of Nazareth willingly gave up his life not for anything he could get out of it, but for the good, the well-being, the welfare, the salvation, the emancipation of others. An old gospel song I remember hearing as a child spoke of his unselfish sacrificial death and sang in the refrain, *'Now that's love'.* The unselfish, sacrificial way of the cross, which is the way of Jesus, is nothing less than the way of the very love of God. Not syrupy sweet or sentimental, but sacrificial. This way of love is the liberating way that leads to real life.

The late Raymond Brown, in his commentary on John's Gospel, notes that this text speaks of love not only in the unselfish way of the cross, but in the unselfish way of Christmas.

An ancient Christian hymn now found in Philippians (2: 3–11 NRSV) says that in coming into the world God 'emptied himself' in order to share our lives and to show us the way. I suspect the poet Christina Rossetti realised this when she wrote

> Love came down at Christmas,
> Love all lovely, Love Divine,
> Love was born at Christmas,
> Star and Angels gave the sign.

This way of Jesus, which is the way of love, can change lives and ultimately can change the world. And the reason is simple. This way of love is nothing less than the way of God, our Creator!

So how do we, as Teilhard de Chardin said, 'harness for God the energies of love'? How do we internalise, organise and mobilise love in such ways that it is let loose in and among us until we all are set free? How do we cultivate and nourish a Jesus-centered life in such ways that his way of love becomes our way of life?

Are there ways, practices, disciplines, tested by time, that can help us to learn the ways of love?

The good news is that the answer is an unequivocal yes!

And it's not rocket science. It's actually quite simple. But it is not easy, because it involves intentional practices for a Jesus-centered life on our part. These choices together are like a formula for how to live: a Rule of Life, if you will. I like to call it the Way of Love.

It's fairly easy to remember: Turn, Learn, Pray, Worship, Bless, Go and Rest.

Turn – pause for a moment, and ask yourself how you might do things differently.

Learn – try reading the Bible a little each day, especially Jesus' life and teachings.

Pray – talk to God each day, in whatever way works best for you.

Worship – visit a local church, maybe with someone who already goes.

Bless – find at least one way to make a difference in someone's life today.

Go – chat with someone who talks or thinks differently from you.

Rest – spend time outside, relax with a book, do something that brings you peace.

When we make simple but intentional choices, then we find that love is in all of it. The struggles that you and I face are real. But oh, that love that comes from God is even more real, and powerful enough to see us through it all. This Christmas, and in the New Year, choose to Turn, Learn, Pray, Worship, Bless, Go and Rest ... And don't forget those who are struggling or suffering this Christmas season. Remember them in your thoughts and prayers every day.

If today you feel more burdened with sadness, grief or worry rather than filled with joyous hope, remember this: God's love is real, God's love is powerful and God's love is there for you.

God love you. God bless you. And may God hold us all, the entire human family and creation, in those almighty hands of love.

Your brother,

Bishop Michael Curry